"With articulate precision and pastoral grace, Aaron Früh in his book *The Decree of Esther* gives us a clear roadmap to a life of personal victory and fruitfulness. He not only details the ways in which the Spirit prepares us for the King, but he offers practical wisdom on how we can walk in overcoming victory amidst the present tensions and anxieties of our age. This is a refreshing book and one that is timely and prophetic for our time."

Steve Fry, senior pastor, Belmont Church; president, Messenger Fellowship; author, *Rekindled Flame*

"Aaron Früh's book goes far beyond the intriguing story line of Esther's life. It opens up new vistas of understanding the Hebrew Scriptures as continually pointing to the coming Messiah. If Jesus is not foreshadowed in the stories of the patriarchs and prophets, then He cannot be the Messiah of Israel and the nations. Aaron understands this and will challenge you to listen to the Holy Spirit as you read the story of this Persian queen."

Don Finto, pastor emeritus, speaker and author

"There are power truths layered between the lines written in the account of Esther for those who dare to dig beneath the surface of her story. Aaron Früh brings the hidden things to life in this deep exploration of principles that will not only bless you but liberate you to experience another level of blessing in your own life."

Michelle McKinney Hammond, author of *The Power of Being a Woman*

"Pastor Aaron Früh's *Decree of Esther* is a timely and revealing book that illustrates how just one person can make a difference. Faced by overwhelming odds, Esther was faithful, courageous and obedient in carrying out God's plan for her life, thereby liberating the Jews of Persia. Pastor Früh's in-depth study and unique analysis provide encouragement for the faithful that God is in control."

Stuart J. Roth, senior counsel,
American Center for Law and Justice

"This is a book full of vital truth that will set you free and cause you to gain the victory over your enemies. If any Christian, whether a minister or church member, is not living in peace and victory within and without, there is a missing ingredient in his or her formula for victorious living. The truth revealed in this book concerning spoken and written decrees could be that missing ingredient.

"In my fifty years of ministry, I have practiced this truth in maintaining my personal life, family and ministry. Much of the advancement we have made in pioneering the full restoration of Christ's fivefold ministries can be attributed to practicing the principles and truths found in this book. We called them 'apostolic decrees' and 'prophetic proclamations.'

"Aaron uses life and biblical examples to prove that every Christian can have this same power in his or her life. If you, like Esther, learn to make the proper preparation, practice the right principles, develop Christ's attitude and take the prescribed biblical action, then you can defeat all your enemies and live the victorious life. This book is necessary reading for every Christian who wants to be free, holy, victorious and prosperous. Like Esther, you will gain victory not only for yourself but for many of God's people."

Dr. Bill Hamon, chairman, founder and bishop,
Christian International Ministries Network;
president, Christian International College

THE DECREE OF
ESTHER

CHANGING THE FUTURE THROUGH
PROPHETIC PROCLAMATION

AARON FRÜH

Chosen
Grand Rapids, Michigan

© 2004 by Aaron Früh

Published by Chosen Books
A division of Baker Publishing Group
P.O. Box 6287, Grand Rapids, MI 49516-6287
www.chosenbooks.com

Printed in the United States of America

Library of Congress Cataloging-in-Publication Data
Früh, Aaron, 1958–
    The decree of Esther : changing the future through prophetic proclamation / Aaron Früh.
        p.   cm.
    ISBN 0-8007-9374-9 (pbk.)
    1. Bible. O.T. Esther—Criticism, interpretation, etc. 2. Prayer—Biblical teaching. 3. Assertiveness (Psychology)—Biblical teaching. I. Title.
BS1375.6.P68F78 2004
222'.906—dc22   2004014428

I dedicate this book to my late father, William Früh, who imparted to me the passion for dreaming dreams, and to my mother, Nora Früh, who imparted to me the passion for writing them down.

CONTENTS

Acknowledgments

Since this is my first published book, the process of writing it was more than an everyday project I was familiar and comfortable with. It was a new discipline that was in many ways, to a new writer, mountainous in proportion. It would be ludicrous to reach the top of the peak without expressing my thanks and deep gratitude to many friends and family members who carried the water and supplies (and sometimes me!) in my quest for the summit.

Thank you, Sharon, my wife and best friend, for your endless exhortations to me to pick up the writer's pen. It was your belief that I had a writer's gifting that started this journey. This book came out of the reservoir of life experiences that we have walked through together. You are a wonderful example of a modern-day Esther. I love you.

Thank you, Rachel, Elizabeth, Hannah and Nathan—the best children any father could ever hope to have. Your support through this season means more than you will ever know. Thanks for putting up with my temporary "office" on the dining room table!

Thank you, Kathy Watson, for editing the first draft of the manuscript before it was sent to the Chosen Books editors. You made it shine! You are not only a fine journalist but a wonderful sister, and I am so proud of you. Thanks to Stu, your patient husband, who endured lots of meals without you because of my distracting phone calls.

Thank you to the three couples I have been privileged to be mentored by: Bob and Charlene Pagett, Santa Cruz, California; Pastors Paul and Elizabeth Tinlin, Chicago; and Pastors Fred and Nellie Roberts, Durbin, South Africa.

Thank you to the elders and leaders of Knollwood Church, to whom I gladly submit my life: Jim Ott, Danny Sellers, Geoff Vines, Danny Fulkerson, Brian Cuccias and Don Woodward.

Thank you to Knollwood Church. You guys make pastoring a joy!

Thank you to my fellow pastors and church staff who share in the ministry with me. You covered the bases for me so I was free to write. Thanks to Scott and Sandy Williams, Alan and Heidi Pastian, David and Irene Sauger, Scott and Katie Jacobsen Moore, Sandra Guy, Cynthia Thomas, Jim and Sally Cornelson, Karen Greene, Zania Rice and Cain Drieling.

Thank you to Yisrael Stafansky from Jerusalem for your help in researching Purim and for the three books on the subject you hand-delivered.

Thank you to David and Shoshi Boxerman, my grandmother Rose's first cousins, for the many Jewish history lessons around your dinner table in Nes Ziona, Israel.

Thanks to those who have blessed my life by their friendship: Dr. Truett Bobo, Owen Carr, Michelle McKinney Hammond, Sam Huddleston, Neville and Wendy McDonald, Sheryl Merritt, Curt Miller, Bishop Ed Peecher, Stuart and Elizabeth Roth, Steve Savelich and Rich Valkenet.

Thanks to Bishop Luther Blackwell, who inspired the theme of this book. Your preaching the pictures, types and shadows of the Scriptures helped me see the book of Esther in a new way.

Thanks to Dick Mills, who first got me started on my quest to study the life of Esther.

Thanks to Lars and Harriet Svensson. No son-in-law has better in-laws than you! Thanks, "Sven," for filling the shoes of my deceased father.

Thanks to my loved ones, Ross and Carol Fruin, Dr. Steve and Gail Lo Bue, Tom Svensson and Dr. Ted and Jane Washburn. My life would have missed a wonderful treasure had you not been in it.

Thanks to Nathan and Nila Früh for the many feasts around your table.

Thank you to Jane Campbell, editorial director of Chosen Books, for your willingness to read my original proposal and your constant guidance along the path to the summit. I will never forget the fact that you gave me this chance. Whether or not I receive another opportunity to publish again with Chosen, I trust we will be lifelong friends.

Thank you to Ann Weinheimer, who edited the final draft. Ann, I sensed through the process that editing for Chosen Books is a ministry for you, and I so appreciated your prayers and words of encouragement.

Last, thanks, Jamey Greene, for asking me about the progress of this book in the church parking lot just after I received my last rejection letter from another publisher. Your question inspired me to give the process of getting published another whirl!

1

BEAUTY ON DISPLAY

To read the book of Esther as a historical account of a musty long-dead king and his queens is to miss a wonderful truth. The Old Testament is a Passion play painted in beautiful typology—that is, pictures or shadows of New Testament truths to come.

When I first read Esther many years ago, I missed the amazing story that unfolds in this book. In fact I missed the whole point of Esther! Builds your confidence in me as your guide through our study, doesn't it?

Don't be alarmed. God gave us the Old Testament not just as a historical reference; He gave it to us to show us how to live in these times, and He is opening these books to blind eyes as never before. You are about to open an ancient treasure that I pray will become a beautiful present-day truth for you as it has for me. Are you ready to begin our journey?

Like many other stories found in the Old Testament, Esther is a "shadow" book—a shadow of things to come. One typical theme runs through the entire book. It may surprise you, but I believe that the book of Esther is actually a prophetic message for end-time saints. In this first chapter I want to unfold for you the central truth in Esther, the truth that will shape our whole study in the pages ahead.

A King, a Bride, a Kingdom

The book of Esther is a story about a king, a bride and a kingdom. Chapter 1 of Esther opens with the dramatic details of the king's dominion. King Ahasuerus is a Persian monarch who rules over 127 provinces from India to Ethiopia. He reigns over the vast Median and Persian empires. At the time of his rule, he is the most powerful man on earth. It is important to note that Israel and all of the Jews living in Jerusalem at the time are a part of his empire.

In the third year of Ahasuerus' reign he throws a feast for all of his officials and servants. Look at the splendor of his majesty's taste:

He showed the riches of his glorious kingdom and the splendor of his excellent majesty for many days, one hundred and eighty days in all. And when these days were completed, the king made a feast lasting seven days for all the people who were present in Shushan the citadel, from great to small, in the court of the garden of the king's palace. There were white and blue linen curtains fastened with cords of fine linen and purple on silver rods and marble pillars; and the couches were of gold and silver on a mosaic pavement of alabaster, turquoise, and white and black marble. And they served drinks in golden vessels, each

14

vessel being different from the other, with royal wine in abundance, according to the generosity of the king.

Esther 1:4–7

After the 180-day feast for the royals, the king then throws a seven-day party for everyone in the capital city of Shushan, both great and small. Throughout these celebrations the king has displayed "the riches of his glorious kingdom and the splendor of his excellent majesty." Then on the seventh day of the second feast King Ahasuerus decides to bring out the crown jewel of his kingdom. He desires to display his bride, Queen Vashti, so that everyone can see her glorious beauty:

> On the seventh day, when the heart of the king was merry with wine, he commanded Mehuman, Biztha, Harbona, Bigtha, Abagtha, Zethar, and Carcas, seven eunuchs who served in the presence of King Ahasuerus, to bring Queen Vashti before the king, wearing her royal crown, in order to show her beauty to the people and the officials, for she was beautiful to behold.

Esther 1:10–11

Perhaps surprising everyone in attendance, Queen Vashti refuses the king's request. Her reason is not stated. Some think that she refused to appear before the king because servants delivered his request and not the king himself. I think we can assume, though, that sending a message by a servant was a fairly standard procedure in a large royal household.

Some believe that because the king was "merry with wine" perhaps he requested not only the unveiling of her beauty but her royal robe as well. Thus she chose rightfully not to be publicly humiliated.

I do not pick that up from the passage or from the king's behavior. We may infer, for instance, that he is a good host. He invites the great and the small to his banquet, and verse 8 tells us, "In accordance with the law, the drinking was not compulsory; for so the king had ordered all the officers of his household, that they should do according to each man's pleasure." Ahasuerus appears to be generous—not a control freak. To me the king seems like a reasonable, honorable man, and asking his wife to take off her clothes in public would be demeaning to him as well.

Whatever her reason, the queen does not comply and it upsets the king.

> Queen Vashti refused to come at the king's command brought by his eunuchs; therefore the king was furious, and his anger burned within him.
>
> Esther 1:12

Now the king has a problem. It is the last day of his feasts and he wants the capital city to see his beautiful bride, but she refuses. What's a king to do? Ahasuerus gathers together his wise men and asks them a question:

> "What shall we do to Queen Vashti, according to law, because she did not obey the command of King Ahasuerus brought to her by the eunuchs?"
>
> Esther 1:15

One of the wise men has an answer:

> And Memucan answered before the king and the princes: "Queen Vashti has not only wronged the king, but also all the princes, and all the people who are in all the provinces

16

of King Ahasuerus. . . . If it pleases the king, let a royal decree go out from him, and let it be recorded in the laws of the Persians and the Medes, so that it will not be altered, that Vashti shall come no more before King Ahasuerus; and let the king give her royal position to another who is better than she."

Esther 1:16, 19

The decision is made. Vashti will no longer come before the king and her position will be given to another. Chapter 2 of Esther picks up with this new problem facing the king: Vashti is long gone, and he is lonely for a beautiful queen. His servants provide further direction:

After these things, when the wrath of King Ahasuerus subsided, he remembered Vashti, what she had done, and what had been decreed against her. Then the king's servants who attended him said: "Let beautiful young virgins be sought for the king; and let the king appoint officers in all the provinces of his kingdom, that they may gather all the beautiful young virgins to Shushan the citadel, into the women's quarters, under the custody of Hegai the king's eunuch, custodian of the women. And let beauty preparations be given them. Then let the young woman who pleases the king be queen instead of Vashti." This thing pleased the king, and he did so.

Esther 2:1–4

The young women chosen for the Persian kingdom's beauty contest are to be given "beauty preparations." Remember, the book of Esther is a story of a king, a bride and a kingdom. It is a story that begins with a king who wants to display the glory of his bride, the crown jewel of his kingdom . . . on the last day.

17

Making the Connection

Are you beginning to see the application of this amazing story?

The New Testament addresses this Old Testament foreshadowing in Ephesians 5:27. Speaking of the Bride of Christ, the Church, Paul the apostle says that Christ gave Himself for the Church "that He might present it to Himself a glorious church, not having spot or wrinkle or any such thing, but that it should be holy and without blemish."

We see the connection again in Revelation 19:7: "Let us be glad and rejoice and give Him glory, for the marriage of the Lamb has come, and His wife has made herself ready."

Many in the Church today are talking about "the last days." We ponder so many things: Who is the Antichrist? What is the significance of the number 666? Who are the four horsemen of the apocalypse? When does the Rapture of the Church take place? Will the Temple in Israel be rebuilt?

I am a student of biblical prophecy myself, but I think we miss the point entirely if we fail to see what Christ is mainly concerned with in this final chapter of time. He is a King who wants to display to the world the glory of His Bride, the Church, the crown jewel of His majestic Kingdom.

In this last day of time, King Jesus is calling His Bride to display her beauty to the world. Christ is returning for a beautiful Bride.

A Kingdom Book

The book of Esther is not only a shadow of things to come; it is a Kingdom book. That is, through it we glean insight into how God's government operates, its order, its protocol. In these early pages He is teaching us about purification.

The King James Version of the Bible translates Esther 2:3 this way: "Let their things for purification be given them." In this time of maturing and purification, our King is sanctifying His Bride and removing all of our blemishes and stains. He is giving us the things for our purification.

In Esther 2:12 we get a glimpse of what the beautification process was like for these girls who would be brought before the king:

> Each young woman's turn came to go in to King Ahasuerus after she had completed twelve months' preparation, according to the regulations for the women, for thus were the days of their preparation apportioned: six months with oil of myrrh, and six months with perfumes and preparations for beautifying women.

Every young woman who desired to stand before the king was required to complete twelve months of beauty treatments. The number twelve is the scriptural number of authority, order and power. The children of Israel were organized into twelve tribes. There were twelve apostles and there are twelve gates into the city of heaven. Twelve speaks of order and protocol.

I have emphasized that King Ahasuerus desired to display his bride's glory on the seventh day of the feast. Why the seventh day? The significance of this number as well seems to enhance the principle of purification.

The number seven is associated with the Kingdom of God throughout the Bible. It is the number of perfection and completion. *Seven* is a joining of the numbers *three* and *four*. *Three* signifies the Trinity, Father, Son and Holy

Spirit: Jesus is Lord of heaven. *Four* is a universal number and represents the four corners of the earth: Jesus is Lord of the earth. Christ our King is Lord of heaven and Lord of the earth.

The king desires to display the beauty of his bride on the seventh day. The Bride of Christ is coming into her time of perfection and completion, and the Lord of heaven and the earth is calling her to make herself ready. "[Christ equips us] till we all come to the unity of the faith and the knowledge of the Son of God, to a perfect man, to the measure of the stature of the fullness of Christ" (Ephesians 4:13).

Following Kingdom Protocol

Too often we saints try to look irresistibly attractive to the world *before* we follow the beauty preparation requirements of the Kingdom. As a result, our mascara is smudged, our socks have holes and our hair is tangled.

Yet on we rush. Today's beauty business is a multi-billion-dollar industry. In the last twelve months, we Americans spent $483 million in search of the perfect tan. To shampoo our hair, we spent $1.79 billion. To condition our hair, we spent another $1.1 billion. Cosmetic sales top $5 billion each year. We men spend more than $700 million a year on fragrances. And let's not leave out the babies! We spend $61 million a year on baby powders, ointments, creams and petroleum jelly. We are willing to spend the dollars because we appreciate things of beauty.

Once we are back home with our foundations, powders and perfumes, we spend countless ages in the application process. Hey, it takes a lot of preparation these days to become presentable to the world. We want to be pleasing to the eye.

Notice the line "And let beauty preparations be given them." The Church can never be the beautiful Bride we were meant to be until we follow Kingdom protocol. We must learn what it means to prepare, to be purified. Then we can comb our hair, fix our makeup and heal—not just cover up—our blemishes.

The King cannot lead us on our final triumphal procession as His light to the world until we do. The King is not going to put you and me on display until we have been prepared.

If we realized the significance of the moment we are living, then we would never miss one experience in our preparation for beauty. Esther did not miss one day. She completed the entire twelve months and then her moment came to be put on display. Her ability to walk in authority as the bride came at the price of long months of preparation and submission to Kingdom protocol.

I wonder if we believers would experience more victory and triumph if we loved the process as much as the procession? Too often we reject the preparation time and expect the triumphal procession. We desire power without preparation and promotion without protocol. Instead of daily being led in triumphal procession as a majestically beautiful Bride that the world would desire to emulate, too many of us are in the stands watching the parade because we did not want to submit to the purification part of the beauty process. Instead of going from glory to glory, we go from headache to heartache.

It is not pretty to witness a believer in constant discouragement. We have been given the keys of the Kingdom, so anything less than a victorious, glorious lifestyle means that we have missed something in the preparation process.

Maybe somewhere on the inside of us is an undercurrent of unwillingness. We do not want to follow Kingdom principles sent from the King Himself or from His servants sent to equip and train us for beauty. The reality is that we will never be put on display until we are willing to be prepared.

This is the seventh day. A day in which Christ is maturing us and bringing us into completion. It is the day of His power. A day in which He is putting things in order under the protocol of His Kingdom's authority.

David says in Psalm 110:3, "Your people shall be volunteers in the day of Your power; in the beauties of holiness, from the womb of the morning."

There is a life of triumph ahead for all those willing to follow the protocol of purification. It is time for the Bride to make herself ready for her final triumphal procession. It's showtime!

THE MYRRH ANOINTING

Maybe you have thought this. At least I know I have. I have thought that somewhere in this beauty process we call the Christian life I have missed something: a lesson on etiquette, a trip to the makeover specialist, a page in the beauty preparation textbook we call the Scriptures.

I mean, let's be honest for a minute. Ladies, spiritually speaking, do you see yourself dressed in New York Saks Fifth Avenue apparel, ready and waiting for your husband to sweep you off your feet and take you to the finest restaurant in, let's say, Paris? Or, spiritually, do you see yourself a few notches below this in a worn-out wool bathrobe frying bacon and eggs for supper? I mean, are you becoming more beautiful spiritually every day or do you sometimes think you missed a key element in the beauty process along the way?

Men, how do you view your progress in becoming more like Jesus? Would you say that spiritually you are a dapper *GQ* man wearing a tuxedo, riding in a limo? Or are you wearing a T-shirt, sucking in a beer belly and driving an old pickup truck?

Ladies and gentlemen, ugliness is not just skin deep. Underneath the bathrobe and T-shirt, we have issues. We cannot seem to get rid of them even though we try. These ugly issues jump out at us when we least expect them to. Indeed, we *have* missed something in the beauty process.

And what is it we are missing? I like to call it the *myrrh anointing*. This special anointing is for everyone who names the name of Christ. Like the king's wish for Esther, Jesus desires for you to have this special anointing. He wants your beauty to be so irresistible that He cannot help but lavish you with His favor. You might be saying right now, "Hey, I thought I bought a book about how to write decrees and make appeals that change my future. Why are we talking about beauty preparations and the oil of myrrh? What does myrrh have to do with writing decrees anyway?"

The climax of Esther's life is the decree she wrote that literally changed the course of a nation. It was the earlier foundational principles she practiced, however, that brought her to the place of authority and power in which she could write this life-giving decree. The first six chapters of our study, then, are foundational in nature. Leave out one principle and the pen of authority will never be placed in your hand. The power of the pen does not reside in the ink but in the character of the person doing the writing.

So, dear reader, stay with me as we see how God led Esther to write a decree that changed her future. My prayer is that if we allow God to mold our character as Esther allowed Him to mold hers, then the decrees we write when we finish this book will be just as effective as Esther's. Are you ready to take a journey into a new arena of faith?

For Esther it all started with the myrrh anointing. If you would like to receive the myrrh anointing, please look with me at Esther's beauty preparation. But I am warning you now. This is not a cushy trip to a day spa.

A Year of Beauty Work

Each young woman who is called to display her beauty to the king has to complete twelve months of beauty preparations.

> Each young woman's turn came to go in to King Ahasuerus after she had completed twelve months' preparation, according to the regulations for the women, for thus were the days of their preparation apportioned: six months with oil of myrrh, and six months with perfumes and preparations for beautifying women.
>
> Esther 2:12

This king is a connoisseur of beauty. He can spot a wrinkle or a blemish from across the room. This beauty contest has much higher rewards than the Miss America contests of our day. The one who captures the king's heart with the display of her beauty will become queen of the most powerful kingdom on earth. With such stakes involved, who would not gladly follow the beauty regulations for twelve months, as arduous as they are?

There can be no procrastination, no time lost. Every pore of the skin must be perfect. Thus begins the strict beauty process: "Six months with oil of myrrh, and six months with perfumes and preparations for beautifying women."

I have to say that this timing bothers me. During the first six months of the process Esther must apply the oil of myrrh. Day in and day out. Application after application. She must soak in it and bathe in it. Each day she arrives at the salon, the myrrh is applied. Can you imagine the monotony of soaking in liquid myrrh each and every day for six months? After the first week there is myrrh in Esther's taste buds, and her food begins to taste like myrrh. Every breath through her nostrils smells like myrrh. Don't worry, Esther! Only five months and three weeks left of liquid myrrh. Only 176 days left to go in the myrrh anointing.

So what is myrrh, anyway? The root of the Hebrew word for *myrrh* is *marah*, which means (are you ready for the irony?) "bitter." As we will learn, myrrh is a mercurial substance. It was an important ingredient in the anointing oil used in the Temple, yet it could turn water bitter. It was a gift to the baby Jesus, yet it was also a powerful drug, and it was there tormenting Christ at His crucifixion. It could embalm bodies and at the same time take away wrinkles.

Before it is made into a liquid, myrrh is a gummy substance that is found in certain trees and shrubs in the Middle East. Inside the bark of the shrub are tear ducts filled with the pale yellow myrrh liquid. When the bark is torn, the liquid myrrh flows freely through the wound and hardens into a reddish-brown nugget about the size of a walnut and shaped like a tear. The hardened tears are harvested and ground down into a powder and later made into a liquid.

Why does the king want his future bride to endure six months of this strange, bitter brew? Why could it not be one month of bitter myrrh and then eleven months of perfumes? Why does it take so much bitterness, in this case half of the time, to become beautiful?

Esther had no choice but to accept the process if she desired a chance for the crown. And should she be so privileged as to receive it, it would truly represent not only glory but also endurance. For every young woman in the contest, it was the crown that made the pain of the preparation worth every second of discomfort.

A Crown Worth the Price

Dear one, it is clear from Scripture that you and I are contending for a crown someday. There are several crowns mentioned in the Bible.

First, the incorruptible crown:

> Do you not know that those who run in a race all run, but one receives the prize? Run in such a way that you may obtain it. And everyone who competes for the prize is temperate in all things. Now they do it to obtain a perishable crown, but we for an imperishable crown.
>
> 1 Corinthians 9:24–25

Next, the crown of righteousness:

> Finally, there is laid up for me the crown of righteousness, which the Lord, the righteous Judge, will give to me on that Day, and not to me only but also to all who have loved His appearing.
>
> 2 Timothy 4:8

Also mentioned in Scripture are the crown of life and the crown of glory. When we see Jesus I am convinced that everyone who has received a crown will join in with the 24 elders and cast the crowns at His feet. Each crown is a reward for some point in your life when you endured hardship and suffering and yet remained faithful to the process of becoming everything God wanted you to become.

So for Esther to complete the process of becoming a beautiful bride without spot or wrinkle or any other blemish, six months of the oil of myrrh was necessary.

Part of my role as pastor is training and equipping young men and women in the ministry. And each one must go through a myrrh anointing. One thing I always stress is that what you are in private is what you are in public. If they have teachable spirits, willing hearts, lives of prayer and commitments to be the priests of their own homes first and foremost, then they will always prosper in public ministry. Most of us will excuse youthful mistakes if we know a leader's heart is pure and he or she is willing to learn from mistakes.

I love the local church and I am humbled to be a pastor. The church is like a laboratory where every day I get the exciting opportunity to examine and study the maturing process of believers. Everyone is at a different stage and season of life. Some are immersed in myrrh while others have graduated to the sweet-smelling fragrance department. Some are on the mountain and some are head over heels in the valley. But God's grace never ceases to amaze me because all of them come through one way or another.

If you take a moment and look back over all of your life experiences you will soon discover that it is those bitter moments, the moments you do not readily welcome, that become the foundation for your beauty. Those are seasons in your life when even your taste buds are filled with the bitterness of myrrh. You bathe in it and soak in it and wish you could put on the finishing touches of your beauty process with cosmetics and perfumes, but an unseen hand continues to apply the oil of myrrh. Take heart, beloved. You are flowing in the myrrh anointing.

The Bitter Season

As odd as it may sound, there is such a season of life. In Esther's case it was half bitter myrrh and half perfumes and cosmetics. Think about your past, and your beauty preparation schedule may be a lot like that.

Even nature shows us that a bitter season must occur. Take the four seasons of the year. Without dark stormy days in the summer, we would have constant sunshine—and the attendant brown and scorched foliage. Without the bitter cold of winter, we would contend with many insects that could prevent the spring and summer harvests from bearing fruit.

The oil of myrrh, the myrrh anointing, is not something we readily embrace. It is the season in life that is bitter and painful. But the season of fruitfulness will not come without a complete immersion in the oil of myrrh.

As the Bible explains, this anointing oil is not composed solely of myrrh. Myrrh is, however, the starting place. God gave detailed instructions of the type and amount of spices used in the oil of anointing.

Moreover the LORD spoke to Moses, saying: "Also take for yourself quality spices—five hundred shekels of liq-

29

uid myrrh, half as much sweet-smelling cinnamon (two hundred and fifty shekels), two hundred and fifty shekels of sweet-smelling cane, five hundred shekels of cassia, according to the shekel of the sanctuary, and a hin of olive oil. And you shall make from these a holy anointing oil, an ointment compounded according to the art of the perfumer. It shall be a holy anointing oil."

Exodus 30:22–25

If you desire to walk in complete anointing, you must start with the oil of myrrh. You must begin the process with the things you would rather avoid. The apostle Peter says, "But may the God of all grace, who called us to His eternal glory by Christ Jesus, after you have suffered a while, perfect, establish, strengthen, and settle you" (1 Peter 5:10).

The suffering that I am speaking about here is not necessarily a time of being persecuted for righteousness sake, or being misunderstood or even hated because of your faith in Christ. For me the myrrh season is a time when God is cutting through the outer layers of my heart and grinding down the residue of my callousness that is keeping me from His favor. It is a season when God by His mercy has revealed to me some issues that need correction and healing and I am (sometimes reluctantly) submitting to the process of maturity. It is the season when God takes my hardened tears, grinds them down and turns them into free-flowing tears of rejoicing. It is the season when God heals my wounds that caused my tears to be hardened in the first place.

Myrrh was a very expensive commodity in the ancient world. It is mentioned in the Bible more than twenty times. Here are some of the uses for myrrh. See if you can find any spiritual connection. It was believed that myrrh cured

30

stretch marks, athlete's foot, impaired digestion, weakened immune systems, mouth ulcers, bad breath (I think our wagging tongues often need a good dose of the myrrh anointing—how about you?), sore throats and chapped and cracked skin. Some believe that it was one of the most sought after medicines in the world. Though bitter to the taste it carried healing qualities.

Don't Skip the Myrrh Season

Your myrrh season will not be over in a day. The myrrh anointing took six months for Esther. Too often we are concerned with the last six months of the beauty process. We want to hurry in our journeys to the season of maturity when we get to choose fragrant perfume or fancy aftershave lotion or a complimentary shade of lipstick.

Lots of people wonder why life cannot be just a little smoother. Does it seem you are blessed for a season and then your imperfections overcome you? I am not a cosmetologist but I think I can help you. What has happened is that you started with the blush and eye shadow, and you have no foundation to build on.

The foundation is actually more important than the visible finishing touches. The foundation covers imperfections and blemishes. It fills the lines and creases and hides age spots and broken blood vessels.

So first you apply foundation; without it you do not have a smooth surface to build upon. Likewise you first must be anointed with myrrh.

I am impressed with the lives and testimonies of great Christian leaders throughout the ages. I love to read the biographies of godly men and women who achieved great things for God. Generally I find that one line of truth is woven through all of their accounts: Each in his or her own way endured years and years of patient endurance and humble sacrifice. Many of us would like to bypass that season, but it is the very thing that lays the foundation for the time when God displays us as His beautiful Bride.

It is because of this desire to skip the tough stuff that many believers do not last long as overcoming Christians. They have beautiful gifts and they even look good and smell good, but somewhere in the process they avoided the oil of myrrh. They ended the painful maturity process of their faith to enjoy the instant pleasures of life. This beauty really is only skin deep. When the perfume and powder wear away, their faces will reveal wrinkles, age spots, unhealed blemishes—issues that have never received the myrrh anointing.

Remember, Esther is a shadow book. It is the story of a King in search of a beautiful Bride. One day the Church will be presented to Jesus as a "glorious church, not having spot or wrinkle or any such thing, but that it should be holy and without blemish" (Ephesians 5:27).

The Lord Himself is preparing us for this glorious moment when we see Him face to face in all of His wonder and majesty. He is anointing us with myrrh in order to remove the age spots caused by the curse of sin. His myrrh anointing is erasing the wrinkles and blemishes caused by fear and is covering and healing the broken blood vessels caused by stress and pain. Take heart. Jesus is preparing us for a glorious wedding banquet, and until that day dawns He will continue to transform us into His image.

But we all, with unveiled face, beholding as in a mirror the glory of the Lord, are being transformed into the same image from glory to glory, just as by the Spirit of the Lord.

2 Corinthians 3:18

A Sweet Smell

Myrrh was used, as we have seen, as an aid to beauty by healing blemishes. It also contributed to fragrance: As a preservative, it kept things from rotting. Without the oil of myrrh in our lives our anointing would put off a foul odor. To say it plainly, we would stink.

Paul makes it clear that each of us should be like a sweet-smelling fragrance and preservative in the rotting and decaying world around us:

Now thanks be to God who always leads us in triumph in Christ, and through us diffuses the fragrance of His knowledge in every place. For we are to God the fragrance of Christ among those who are being saved and among those who are perishing.

2 Corinthians 2:14–15

Esther is a Persian name, but this young woman was Jewish and thus also had a Hebrew name. She was probably given a Persian name to disguise her background when living away from her homeland. Esther's Hebrew name is Hadassah. Want to know its meaning? "Fragrance of the myrtle tree." Even Esther's name speaks prophetically of the Church's role as God's sweet-smelling fragrance to the world around us.

Without the element of myrrh in our anointing it will smell sweet for a while, but then it will begin to put off a putrid odor. Remember that there were five hundred shekels of myrrh used in the mixture for anointing oil. If we leave it out, our anointing will be counterfeit and we will never have complete authority to break the issues of bondage in our lives. Isaiah said that "the yoke will be destroyed because of the anointing oil" (Isaiah 10:27).

Myrrh was also used as an embalming spice. Joseph of Arimathea used a one-hundred-pound mixture of myrrh and other spices in the burial of Jesus. Even as the oil of myrrh strengthens the foundations of our lives and helps us walk in the fragrance of Christ, so it anoints the old nature for burial. From time to time God will see in us a new wrinkle or blemish that needs anointing. It is an area that has not yet been buried with Christ. So the unseen hand of the Holy Spirit must come and anoint us with myrrh.

If you are in a time when you are dying to some old attitudes and issues, take heart: Your old self is simply being anointed for burial.

> Therefore we were buried with Him through baptism into death, that just as Christ was raised from the dead by the glory of the Father, even so we also should walk in newness of life. For if we have been united together in the likeness of His death, certainly we also shall be in the likeness of His resurrection.
>
> Romans 6:4–5

In the beautiful typology of Christ and His Bride given in the Song of Solomon, there is a wonderful picture of what happens when we open our hearts to Christ:

> My beloved put his hand by the latch of the door, and my heart yearned for him. I arose to open for my beloved,

and my hands dripped with myrrh, my fingers with liquid myrrh, on the handles of the lock.

Song of Solomon 5:4–5

You see, you cannot open the door of your heart to Jesus without having your hand covered with myrrh. As He is, so we must be. If Jesus bears the marks of suffering and glory, myrrh and perfume, pain and pleasure, so must we. It is a foundational principle of our faith. "If [we are] children, then heirs—heirs of God and joint heirs with Christ, if indeed we suffer with Him, that we may also be glorified together" (Romans 8:17).

I believe it is entirely possible for a person to become a Christian and yet never fully encounter Christ, resulting in a life that never appropriates the full work of the cross for every issue of life. What concerns a pastor more than anything is to see people year after year who never change. They continue to be bound with the same issues. Oh, they are not involved in deep sins or destructive habits; they are just not growing. They are just not becoming more beautiful. They are comfortable with the wrinkles and blemishes. The cross is merely a one-time event in their lives.

But what do we do with Paul who said, "I die daily" (1 Corinthians 15:31)? Or with this statement of Jesus: "If anyone desires to come after Me, let him deny himself, and take up his cross daily, and follow Me" (Luke 9:23)?

Encountering Jesus and the power of His cross is not just a one-time event; it is an every day experience for every believer.

Dear saint, we are living in the last times. Jesus is standing at your heart's door and knocking. Will you take hold of the handle dripping with myrrh and allow the Son of God to come in? Will you encounter Him fully in His death, burial and resurrection? Will you ask the living Lord Jesus to anoint your old nature—wrinkles, age spots and all—with the oil of myrrh? It is the only way you will become the beautiful Bride the King longs to see.

The Cross Turns Bitter to Sweet

I want to discuss further the message of myrrh as it relates to the cross, because one of the last lessons Jesus taught us during His life here on earth involved myrrh.

In fact I used to feel confused by it because Scripture seems to offer contradictory information. Mark 15:23 says, "They gave Him wine mingled with myrrh to drink, but He did not take it." Matthew gives a similar account adding, "When He had tasted it, He would not drink" (27:34). Yet John's gospel says this:

> After this, Jesus, knowing that all things were now accomplished, that the Scripture might be fulfilled, said, "I thirst!" Now a vessel full of sour wine [a mixture of myrrh and wine] was sitting there; and they filled a sponge with sour wine, put it on hyssop, and put it to His mouth. So when Jesus had received the sour wine, He said, "It is finished!" And bowing His head, He gave up His spirit.
>
> John 19:28–30

Who is right? Mark says that Jesus would not drink the myrrh but John says that He did. On closer examination we see that both are right. There were two different times that Christ was offered bitter myrrh to drink at Golgotha, the place of the skull.

The first time, recorded in Mark 15:23 and Matthew 27:34, was before He was crucified. It was Roman custom to offer the victim of crucifixion myrrh mingled with wine before they pierced the hands and feet with the nails. You see, myrrh and wine mixed together act as a stimulant and pain reliever. Jesus rejected the medication so that He would experience the inferno of pain for us. Soon all of the shame, anguish and bitter seasons of our lives would be cast upon Him, and He chose to take the full force of them.

The book of Exodus gives a beautiful foreshadowing of Christ rejecting the numbing myrrh. The children of Israel have crossed the Red Sea triumphantly and have seen their enemies perish before them as the seawalls cascaded down upon the Egyptian horses and chariots. The Israelites sang the song of Moses, and Miriam led a joyful procession of praise with timbrels and dancing. The very next stop in their journey was the wilderness of Shur where for three days they found no water.

> Now when they came to Marah, they could not drink the waters of Marah, for they were bitter. Therefore the name of it was called Marah. And the people murmured against Moses, saying, "What shall we drink?" So he cried out to the Lord, and the Lord showed him a tree; and when he cast it into the waters, the waters were made sweet.
>
> Exodus 15:23–25

Remember, the Hebrew root word for *myrrh* is *marah*, which means "bitter." When the Israelites tasted the bitter water they spat it out, just as Jesus would reject the bitter myrrh after He had tasted it.

Here is the lesson He was teaching us. When we come to the "bitter water" seasons of our lives, we can begin to put the pieces of the puzzle together. First of all, we conclude that we are in the beginning of a myrrh season. Next, we realize that we are thirsty. And finally, we conclude that the water is bitter. Thus we refuse to drink. We mistakenly reject the discomfort of the myrrh in hopes that we can make it to a place where the water is sweet. The Israelites, too, were pressing on to a better place: Elim, where there were twelve wells of fresh water and seventy palm trees for shade. We choose to spit out the bitter myrrh of Shur in order to taste the cool waters of Elim.

Do not think, however, there is any way around those bitter waters without the cross of Christ. Like the tree Moses threw into the water, the tree of Calvary, where Jesus bore our sorrows, is the only way to end our wilderness experience. It is only through the work of the cross that our bitter waters will be made sweet. Without the cross, we are forever stranded in the wilderness. We can never get to Elim and rest . . . and beauty.

God has designed and organized your beauty preparation schedule. Every person's path is different. There are times when, like Esther, you come to a season of life in which all you see, taste and smell seems painfully bitter. How will you endure it? Not by longing for the sweet wells and shade of another season. You simply need to find the one "tree" in your puzzling wilderness that will make your life complete. On that tree Jesus took all of our pain and bitterness. He spat out the myrrh so that He could endure every aspect of our desperate moments. He spat out the myrrh so that when we face our own myrrh anointing we can be transformed into His image—a Church without blot or blemish.

You see, the tree of Calvary, when applied to my bitter wilderness experience, makes it sweet. Jesus has taken away the bitterness of life's suffering. Paul tells us that on the cross Jesus brought us a glorious victory so now we can proclaim, "Death is swallowed up in victory. O Death, where is your sting? O Hades, where is your victory?" (1 Corinthians 15:54–55).

Jesus swallowed the bitterness of death for us and made life sweet. Even your pain is bearable because of the tree of Calvary.

Mark's gospel records that even before the nails pierced Jesus' body, He spat out the myrrh mixed with wine because it acted as a pain reliever and He desired to experience all of our pain. In John's gospel, and also in Matthew 27:48, as we read earlier, Jesus drank the wine mixed with myrrh just before He gave up His spirit. So the last thing Jesus did before He died was to drink the cup of bitterness on our behalf. This was done to fulfill the Scripture, "They also gave me gall for my food, and for my thirst they gave me vinegar to drink" (Psalm 69:21).

Jesus is returning for a glorious Church without stain or wrinkle or any other blemish. And every time we allow the Lord Jesus to anoint us with myrrh to cause us to be more attractive to Him, we are fulfilling the Scriptures.

In the Old Covenant law in Leviticus 14, a procedure is given for cleansing lepers. The priest was to take hyssop (a long reed) and dip it into the blood of an animal and then sprinkle the blood on the hyssop over the leper. David says in Psalm 51:7, "Purge me with hyssop, and I shall be clean; wash me, and I shall be whiter than snow."

Unknowingly, that Roman soldier at Golgotha was fulfilling Levitical law. He took hyssop and put a sponge filled with myrrh on the tip of it and gave it to Christ to drink. Before Jesus committed His spirit into the hands of His Father He was purged with hyssop and anointed with myrrh. We remember, of course, that when Christ came into the world as a baby He was anointed with the gift of myrrh given by the Wise Men. It was used as a balm for the skin care of a new child. Before He gave up His spirit on the cross Jesus was again anointed with myrrh.

Before you give up your spirit, before you give up hope, receive the myrrh anointing. Jesus did. And with that anointing in the wilderness experience of the cross He became gloriously beautiful to God. Because Jesus was cleansed with hyssop and anointed with myrrh, He walked in full authority as He marched into hell and set the captives free. Afterward He ascended into heaven and sat down at the right hand of God the Father.

First the suffering, then the glory. First the bitter, then the sweet. All of the authority that Esther will later receive is a direct result of her willingness to be anointed with myrrh. Beloved, it is time to start walking in divine authority. It is time to get the putrid odor out of our anointing.

The writer of Hebrews says of Jesus,

> In the days of His flesh, when He had offered up prayers and supplications, with vehement cries and tears to Him who was able to save Him from death, and [He] was heard because of His godly fear, though He was a Son, yet He learned obedience by the things which He suffered.
>
> Hebrews 5:7–8

If Jesus learned obedience to God through the things He suffered, then our life journeys will also have moments of myrrh. If Jesus came into the world anointed with myrrh and went out of the world anointed with myrrh, then I say, "Bathe me, Jesus, in the myrrh anointing. I desire to be beautiful and carry with me Your sweet-smelling fragrance."

3

OBEDIENCE IN TWO DIMENSIONS

We all love "rags to riches" stories. The hook that snags us in the checkout line magazine rack is usually baited with a human-interest story of some kind. I have fallen prey from time to time, I admit. No, I am not talking about the tabloid stories of Elvis spottings or invaders from outer space posing as U.S. congressmen. I am talking about those great stories of common people who do uncommon things.

Whether it is an act of heroism that graces the cover of *Reader's Digest*, or a *People* magazine story highlighting the life of a leader who rose from humble beginnings, we are all drawn to these stories. I think what we really want to know is, how did they do it? We want to read between the lines, scouring the story for the fuel that powered their progress. To be honest, sometimes I find myself looking cynically for any "under-the-table" perks they may have received along the way to stardom. "Ah, see there—he won the lottery." Or, "Her family name made her a natural for public promotion." But the human-interest stories that thrill us are those unexplainable rags-to-riches, zero-to-hero, obscure-to-household-name people who come out of nowhere like a brushfire and, in their short moment of history, change the world.

When you study these uncommon lives you find that nothing happened to them by chance. No one handed them a free ticket to achievement. You will find woven into the fabric of their struggles a rite of passage. A time when they faced impossible odds and could easily have retreated and let the moment pass by.

The great leaders of the Bible who changed the world in their time all had a rite-of-passage moment, too. For Abraham, it was leaving his homeland. For Moses, it was the burning bush. For Deborah, it was leading an army when no one else would. For Joseph, it was running from Potiphar's wife. For Elijah, it was Mount Carmel. For David, it was holding back his sword from touching the Lord's anointed. For Daniel, it was praying at his window when he was forbidden to. For Mary, it was believing the message of Gabriel. For Peter, James and John, it was casting the net on the other side of the boat. For Paul, it was the Damascus road.

Esther's Moment

As we study the life of Esther we find that she also has a rite-of-passage moment. And because of her response to it, like other great leaders of the Bible, she passes from obscurity into the spotlight of bountiful favor.

Esther obtains favor in her life, and at a quick glance we might assume that it is because of her beauty. But all of the young women who are being prepared to meet the king are beautiful. Esther has tough competition. It is like a Miss Universe contest. And we know that her road to national legend is not paved with her family lineage. She is a Jewess in a Persian world. Anti-Semitism then was worse than it is today.

What is it, then, that causes favor to flow toward Esther and raise her up above the other women? Our first glimpse into Esther's rite-of-passage moment is found in Esther 2:9–10, when Hegai, the king's man in charge of all the beauty contestants, likes what he sees in Esther.

> Now the young woman pleased him, and she obtained his favor; so he readily gave beauty preparations to her, besides her allowance. Then seven choice maidservants were provided for her from the king's palace, and he moved her and her maidservants to the best place in the house of the women. Esther had not revealed her people or kindred, for Mordecai had charged her not to reveal it.

Here is our answer. It may be true that Esther approaches the threshold of favor by her beauty, but she crosses it only because of her obedience. Mordecai instructs Esther to keep her lineage a secret. Esther obeys. This one act of obedience is like a parenthesis in the story. It almost seems to be out of place here but it is not. The writer tells us that Esther is moved to the best place in the house for the women and then informs us that she has been walking in obedience to the man who had raised her as his own daughter. God places his hand of favor upon Esther and causes her to be promoted because she is obedient.

You see, favor and obedience always go hand in hand. You cannot have one without the other. Let's move on in Esther's progress in the palace and see how she continues to grow in favor.

After Esther's twelve months of preparation are complete she is presented to the king:

> Thus prepared, each young woman went to the king, and she was given whatever she desired to take with her from the women's quarters to the king's palace.
>
> Esther 2:13

Each young woman can take whatever she desires with her when her turn comes to be presented to the king as a candidate for royalty. Imagine the advice from all circles: "That blue dress is most becoming on you"; "The perfume from the Arabian Sea is the scent of choice these days, you know"; "That mineral-rich lotion from the Dead Sea region is not the hot seller right now, so be careful with that one, dear." Each one has lots of clothing and perfume choices. So what does Esther do?

> Now when the turn came for Esther the daughter of Abihail the uncle of Mordecai, who had taken her as his daughter, to go in to the king, she requested nothing but what Hegai the king's eunuch, the custodian of the women, advised. And Esther obtained favor in the sight of all who saw her.
>
> Esther 2:15

When Esther's turn comes, she tunes out all of the voices. The other girls take whatever they desire, but Esther places her desires in alignment with Hegai's advice. She submits

46

her desires to her direct authority, Hegai, the custodian over her life. Do you think it is any accident, then, that verse 15 concludes, "And Esther obtained favor"? You see, we often miss this truth and never receive the right to move into favor. Obedience is our right of passage.

And where does it lead? To the throne.

> The king loved Esther more than all the other women, and she obtained grace and favor in his sight more than all the virgins; so he set the royal crown upon her head and made her queen instead of Vashti.
>
> Esther 2:17

Esther is chosen above all others and crowned queen. It is the epitome of favor given by the hand of a powerful king. And now that she has reached her goal and ascended the throne, does her obedience end? Let's see.

> Now Esther had not yet revealed her kindred and her people, just as Mordecai had charged her, for Esther obeyed the command of Mordecai as when she was brought up by him.
>
> Esther 2:20

At this point she is queen. She could easily say to Mordecai, "Bug off." Other than the king, no one in the empire has the right to command the queen of Persia to do anything. But Esther has a childlike, submitted heart and it is her ticket to favor. Much like David's "I won't touch the Lord's anointed" and Paul's "What would You have me do?" and Peter's "Because You say so, Lord," Esther navigates her right of passage successfully because she has childlike obedience.

And this is still the case for anyone wanting to obtain uncommon favor today. But there is more to learn.

Don't Hide in Your Robe

You know, a funny thing happens when we reach the Kingdom. The royal robes of our newfound faith can, in time, deceive us if we are not careful. These beautiful robes, signifying kingship and priesthood, are a sign of our completion and position in Christ. They are not shields that prevent others from getting close enough to see our flaws and speak words of correction to us.

King David is so dramatically favored that God says no other man ever had a heart like his. Pretty convincing testimony from the One who distributes all the favor, wouldn't you say? David gets the endorsement because, like Esther, his robe never becomes a locked door to an outside voice of appeal. When Nathan points the finger of judgment at him and says, "Thou art the man," David quickly surrenders and repents of his sins of adultery and murder. To me what is so remarkable about this story is not David's quick response but that Nathan feels the freedom to point God's finger of judgment at him without fear of reprisal. Even as king, with all the pomp and circumstance of the palace, David is still the little shepherd boy at heart.

Remember earlier in his life when the Ark of the Covenant is brought back to Jerusalem and off go the robes of royalty as David dances publicly before the Lord. God loves a childlike heart! Be careful that your Christianity does not become so dignified that your royal robes become symbols of what you know rather than symbols of who you are. If they should become symbols only of what you know about God and what you are accomplishing for God, then others will feel awkward in breaking through your "royal highness" outer shell in order to speak the truth in love to your heart buried somewhere under the folds of religiosity. At this dangerous place, Christians are willing to listen only to those who tell them what they want to hear.

This, then, is Esther's secret to favor. She is queen but she relates to Mordecai with a childlike heart just as she did when she was a young girl. So, beloved, if you want to be greatly favored, don't let your heart get haughty in your robes. "Therefore whoever humbles himself as this little child is the greatest in the kingdom of heaven" (Matthew 18:4).

Two-Dimensional Obedience

There is further insight in Esther's obedience. She reaches the palace because she submits her life to her earthly custodians, Mordecai and Hegai.

She then obtains the favor of the king because her heart is in submission to his lordship. King Ahasuerus is not a complete representation of God the Father, of course, but in many ways we can see how Esther's desire to obtain his favor helps guide us in our desire to obtain God's favor. The word *ahasuerus* is not actually a personal name. It is a title like *president* or *emperor* and it means "The Venerable Father."

If we see him as representative of God the Father, then we see that Esther's obedience is two-dimensional. She submits herself both to God, symbolically, and to man. So it is not a surprise that she obtains the favor of both God and man.

You know, as a pastor I so often see dear ones who struggle continuously with this issue and wonder why they cannot seem to obtain favor. It usually boils down to the fact that their obedience is merely one-dimensional.

Some of these individuals, for instance, submit to God but want no part of submission to any earthly authorities, such as parents or counselors or doctors or pastors. When I ask about this they usually say, "Oh, I'm submitted to Christ the King only, not to man." I know that with this one-dimensional obedience it will not be long before they crash and burn. Others are submitted to earthly authorities but they, too, miss the mark. Even though they act like model Christians, their hearts are far from submission to God. And then they wonder why, with all of their Christian works and good deeds, life is crumbling about them. The rite of passage for each person seeking to experience a life of favor is paved with obedience in two dimensions: a childlike, willing heart that is submitted to both God and man.

There is a remarkable passage of Scripture that discloses an event from Jesus' early life. In it we see that His rite of passage is also paved with obedience in two dimensions.

> So when they saw Him, they were amazed; and His mother said to Him, "Son, why have you done this to us? Look, Your father and I have sought You anxiously." And He said to them, "Why is it that you sought Me? Did you not know that I must be about My Father's business?" But they did not understand the statement which He spoke to them. Then He went down with them and came to Nazareth, and was subject to them, but His mother kept all these things in her heart. And Jesus increased in wisdom and stature, and in favor with God and men.
>
> Luke 2:48–52

Notice here that Jesus is in right relationship with His Father: "I must be about My Father's business." And He is in right relationship with His earthly authorities: "He went down with them . . . and was subject to them." Christ, the God-man, found it completely necessary to walk in two-dimensional obedience in order to obtain favor.

The result of His obedience is found in the first three words of the next verse, "And Jesus increased. . . . " Today everyone wants to increase. We want to enlarge our borders, expand our horizons and fulfill our destinies. Many in the Church talk about gaining blessing and favor. You are reading this book most likely because you want to grow to heights that you have never reached before.

What is so exciting is that God is responsible for placing these desires within us. Living a favored life of continual increase is not an impossible dream. A favored life can literally fall in your lap if you will simply decide to walk in two-dimensional obedience. It is no wonder that Jesus increased in wisdom and stature and in favor with God and man. He caused it to happen because He submitted Himself to God and man.

Stature is from the Greek word *lēlikia* that speaks about "a particular time of life" as when a person is said to "be of age." Because of His obedience, Jesus "came of age" or entered into His time, so to speak. His rite of passage into that place where favor was ever flowing toward Him came as a result of two-dimensional obedience.

Are you growing in *lēlikia*? Is this your moment in time and place when favor is moving in your direction? Today, like every day, is the day of God's favor. I want to be on God's favor agenda today, don't you? Just like the men and women in the Scriptures who faced their rite-of-passage moments, there are points of time when it's your turn to be stretched. Though frustrating, even painful, it's best to embrace your moment with a childlike, obedient heart.

I can tell you that the richest experience in life is knowing that you are a candidate for divine blessing. Great joy comes from realizing that this is not a passing fancy but a lifelong experience. Psalm 30:5 says that "His favor is for life." Psalm 16:11 says, "You will show me the path of life; in Your presence is fullness of joy; at Your right hand are pleasures forevermore."

So the next time you are in the checkout line and you see the rags-to-riches, human-interest cover story, remember Esther's example of two-dimensional obedience. For the believer, the road to favor is paved with the willingness to obey God and submit to the ones He has graced to lead us.

4

THE FALLACY OF THE PALACE

Part of me wants the story of Esther to end right here. If it did, it would have a fairytale ending. A young orphaned woman living in exile in a foreign land enters a beauty contest. She is given beauty treatments and schooled in the finest traditions in the known world. Amazingly she catches the eye of the king and is swept away to his desert palace to become his wife. Lawrence of Arabia has nothing on the book of Esther! Cinderella and Eliza Doolittle would be proud to let Esther into their sorority of rags-to-riches fairytale characters.

The story does not end here, however, and it is anything but a fairytale. In fact, the harsh realities Esther must endure in order to live a principled, godly life in a foreign land now come crashing in. The blissful promise of a carriage ride to the palace in glass slippers turns into a train ride to the Auschwitz death camp.

Remember, we are still setting the stage and laying the foundation for the true ending of the story—one that is greater than any fairytale. But let's not get ahead of our story. Esther submits to the process of becoming beautiful. She bathes in bitter myrrh and walks in two-dimensional obedience. As a result Esther receives a crown and becomes the center of a great celebration.

> Then the king made a great feast, the Feast of Esther, for all his officials and servants; and he proclaimed a holiday in the provinces and gave gifts according to the generosity of a king.
>
> Esther 2:18

As a result of Esther's faithful obedience she is now walking in royal authority. But she is still living in a foreign land with foreign customs, foreign laws and foreign gods. With royalty comes responsibility. The tension that comes from living in two worlds either produces tenacity or tolerance.

And what of us? Will our generation be known as the generation that learned to coexist with the culture around us or the generation that overcame it? How much are we really willing to tolerate? I believe that the greatest issue for every Christian home today is the "T" word: tolerance. What rating of movies will we tolerate in our homes? Will we go as high as PG? Who will bid PG-13? The R rating is going once, twice. . . . You see we are like the frog in the kettle that slowly comes to a boil. The frog tolerates the rising temperature and does not attempt an escape. Before he knows it he has slowly and systematically tolerated his demise and is boiled to death.

Refusing to Bow

Mordecai, Esther's cousin, is not one to tolerate anything in the world that might compromise his faith. Even though he lives far away from Jerusalem and Temple worship, he does not forget what he stands for.

The third chapter of Esther opens with the promotion of Haman the Agagite above all the other princes in the Persian kingdom. There really is not much significance surrounding that record. Just another rise to prominence of another despot. Not much significance, that is, until we come to Esther 3:2:

> And all the king's servants who were within the king's gate bowed and paid homage to Haman, for so the king had commanded concerning him. But Mordecai would not bow or pay homage.

Houston, we have a problem! King Ahasuerus commands all servants on his payroll to bow to Haman and pay him homage. Among the meanings of the word *homage* are "reverence" and "worship." Mordecai, like the three Hebrew children who would not bow before the golden statue of Nebuchadnezzar, refuses to bow before Haman. For Mordecai this would be breaking the first commandment, "You shall have no other gods before Me," and the second commandment, which instructs us not to bow down to any false god.

Mordecai makes it clear to the other servants why he cannot worship a man:

Then the king's servants who were within the king's gate said to Mordecai, "Why do you transgress the king's command?" Now it happened, when they spoke to him daily and he would not listen to them, that they told it to Haman, to see whether Mordecai's words would stand; for Mordecai had told them that he was a Jew.

Esther 3:3–4

Of what significance is that? Being a Jew means more to Mordecai than ethnicity; it is also his faith. In other words he is saying, "It is contrary to my beliefs to worship a man or a graven image."

At this point any hope of this story ending with "and they all lived happily ever after" is in serious jeopardy. I would suppose that Mordecai was not the only Jew who was a servant within the king's gates. Did other Jews stand with Mordecai or did they succumb to fear? Did a friend approach him and plead with him to give in to Haman? If he did I think the conversation might have gone something like this: "Oh, come on, Mordecai. It's just a little curtsy. God knows you're not actually worshiping this guy Haman—you're just trying to live in harmony and peace and not stir up any controversy. Think about your family, man! Think about that promotion you've been promised. And remember, Mordecai, this guy is an Amalekite. We Jews have been fighting the Amalekites for hundreds of years. There is a lot of bad blood there. If you set him off there is no telling what he might do to you. Besides, things are going well for us in exile. Your cousin Esther, the queen, is going to lobby our cause now. Happy days are here again! *Le'chaim*! To life! We're begging you, Mordecai: Choose life and bow down with the rest of us."

What would you do if you were in Mordecai's shoes? Would you bow or stand? In reality you and I wear Mordecai's shoes every day. The world demands our homage, our attention and our worship. Whatever is our focal point becomes the thing that we worship. Believers today might scoff at the idea of having to bow down and worship powerful people, but what about the more subtle "gods"? Right off the top of my head I can think of two "gods" that tempt and trap believers daily right along with unbelievers: information and entertainment.

We have made a god out of information. Many of us are willing to take the risk of falling into the dark world of Internet pornography, for instance, as blatant pop-up ads and spam flow unbidden across our computer screens. In our desire to be connected to the World Wide Web, have we too often placed information above purity? We have also made a god out of entertainment. Many of us are willing to subject our young children's minds to daily horrors coming through our television sets just so we can have hundreds of channels at our fingertips. How low are we willing to bow to the gods of information and entertainment? How much of this world are we willing to tolerate? Or will we be tenacious like Mordecai and refuse to worship anything that contradicts our principles?

As I said earlier, it is tempting to end the story of Esther right here. The king has found the owner of the lost glass slipper and a Jewish exile is now queen of the kingdom that rules over her people. Things should be looking up now for every Jew in Persia. Now that Esther is queen, their promotion and favor in this alien world is bound to come. Surely they can tolerate a few inconveniences so that their story will have the happy ending we all dream of.

Could it be that we would rather live a fairytale Christianity than face the difficult choices of true Kingdom living?

The Stroke of Midnight

The next two verses quickly bring an end to our fairytale. The stroke of midnight has come and things change dramatically for Esther and all of the Jews living in Persia:

> When Haman saw that Mordecai did not bow or pay him homage, Haman was filled with wrath. But he disdained to lay hands on Mordecai alone, for they had told him of the people of Mordecai. Instead, Haman sought to destroy all the Jews who were throughout the whole kingdom of Ahasuerus—the people of Mordecai.
>
> Esther 3:5–6

Because Mordecai obeys God's law, Haman's wrath is unleashed against the entire Jewish population. He seeks "to destroy all the Jews." Haman and his associates cast "Pur" (lots, like the lots cast at Jesus' crucifixion) to determine the day and the month that they will exterminate the Jews. In our vernacular you could say that they rolled the dice. The time chosen was the thirteenth day of the month of Adar, our March 13.

Once the date of their destruction is determined, Haman brings a false accusation to King Ahasuerus concerning the Jews. Here is the accusation in full:

> Then Haman said to King Ahasuerus, "There is a certain people scattered and dispersed among the people in all the provinces of your kingdom; their laws are different

from all other people's, and they do not keep the king's laws. Therefore it is not fitting for the king to let them remain."

Esther 3:8

Haman is saying, "These people don't belong here. They are from another world and under the laws of another kingdom. They will not abide by the principles of our kingdom. We must, therefore, destroy them." Going one step further, Haman wants to make his accusation law, so he asks the king to put it into writing. Then he adds,

"I will pay ten thousand talents of silver into the hands of those who do the work, to bring it into the king's treasuries." So the king took his signet ring from his hand and gave it to Haman, the son of Hammedatha the Agagite, the enemy of the Jews.

Esther 3:9–10

Haman is described here as "the enemy of the Jews." Later he will be called both an "adversary and enemy" (Esther 7:6). Haman is a type of Satan, the adversary of our souls. Haman's plan is to bribe a band of murderers with ten thousand talents of silver to destroy the Jews, steal their possessions and bring the proceeds into the king's treasuries. Jesus said that Satan has a duplicate mission: "The thief does not come except to steal, and to kill, and to destroy" (John 10:10).

There is a verse in the book of Revelation that has always intrigued me:

Then I heard a loud voice saying in heaven, "Now salvation, and strength, and the kingdom of our God, and the power of His Christ have come, for the accuser of our brethren, who accused them before our God day and night, has been cast down."

Revelation 12:10

I do not understand it, but somehow Satan is standing before God day and night, 24 hours a day, seven days a week, 365 days a year, doing one thing: bringing slanderous accusations against the saints. Perhaps like Haman, Satan and his associates are rolling the dice this very moment and determining what day they are coming to steal your favor and promotion and destroy your future. This very moment, your adversary the devil is breathing out false accusations against you. He is the accuser who never sleeps and he will stop at nothing to destroy you.

No Safety in the Palace

"Oh," you might say, "I'll just bow to Haman and make his accusation and decree go away." It is not that easy. Many Christians live under a fallacy that goes like this: "If I just hide my faith and beliefs under a bushel basket and I don't stand for anything, then I won't need to enter into the spiritual struggle." Ultimately, we believe this approach will protect us from the wrath of Haman. We can live in the safe walls of our fairytale palace without incurring any loss.

Ah, dear saint, think again. As the saying goes, if you stand for nothing you will fall for anything. Remember, we are living in the seventh day, the day in which the King desires to display the beauty of His Bride to the world. Satan despises our beauty and the progress of our faith and has cast his dice against us. But God has cast Satan down to the earth, and he is filled with wrath because he knows that his time is short. Whether you are hiding behind palace walls or not, he has your number.

In our next chapter we will see how Mordecai approaches Queen Esther with the horrifying news of Haman's plans. Mordecai tells Esther the startling reality of the accusation and relays to her an eye-opening warning. He says in essence, "Esther, don't think for one moment that because you're living a fairytale life right now that you are somehow going to be sheltered from the adversary's accusations. Esther, you are a Jew from another world who is called to live by another set of principles, and whether you think you can hide behind the palace walls or not, you are marked with God's name. You won't escape the enemy's accusations and threats." Gulp! That is advice that we all need to hear.

What if Mordecai compromises? What if he backs down from what he knows is right and caves in to the pressure? He and the Jews might enjoy a false sense of peace for a season, and Esther could live comfortably behind her false sense of security within the palace walls. But like the illustration of the unsuspecting frog, they would be in greater and greater danger and they would not notice until it was too late. Mordecai's tolerance for the worship of a false god would slowly wear down his sense of meaning and purpose. If he and his fellow Jews accommodate the pagan cultural belief and practices, their resolve would weaken and before long their consciences would be as good as dead.

In ancient times the city council convened its meetings at the city gates. Many theologians believe that Mordecai held a high position in the government of the Persian capital city of Shushan because it is recorded that he sat at the king's gate. Some believe that he was a magistrate or judge. It is interesting to note that it was at those same gates that Haman was demanding Mordecai's worship. Because of Mordecai's high office, the influence of his decisions would filter down to the Jews in the capital and ultimately to the 127 provinces.

If Mordecai had crumbled in principle at the gates, with all eyes on him, his tolerance of Haman would have spread far and wide in the Jewish community. As go the parents, so go the children. As go the leaders, so goes the nation. Resolve now weakened, senses now numb, what would happen next?

Actually, sometimes nothing. People can live like this for years, bowing to our Hamans every day. We accept those areas of compromise that irritate the conscience but we tolerate them because no one wants to be seen as a "religious nut," a "Jesus freak" or, worse yet, "dogmatic." I do not need to make a list here. Each one of us knows who and what our Hamans are. We might wish secretly that we could muster the tenacity to prevail in the gate of the adversary. But as each new day dawns we become deeper in debt to Haman because we have brokered too many deals with him in order to keep our positions in the gates. So many Christians will never know the spine-tingling rush of choosing to stand when everyone else is bowing.

Please know that Haman's hate for the Jews would not have subsided had Mordecai bowed. It would have only gathered steam as Haman waited for another opportune time to accuse and destroy him.

Righteous Gatekeepers

Note that I am not speaking here about starting a national cultural crusade against sin. I am simply suggesting that the head of every household take up the scepter of leadership right where he or she lives. You are the magistrates, the gatekeepers, the priests of your home. For fathers and mothers it might begin in the video rental store when your kids are putting on the pressure to check out the new PG-13 movie that all of the other kids are watching. Do you want to experience a G-force that is greater than any ride at Universal Studios? Say no! Tell them you have decided not to bow to anything with strong language and sexual content and that as a gatekeeper you are responsible for creating a godly environment. If we do not prevail as gatekeepers in our homes, we lose the opportunity to influence others, especially our children, for righteousness' sake.

How can we speak to the enemy, cancel his plans and write a decree that secures a favored future if our children see us bowing to Haman at the gate?

I have often heard well-intentioned believers quote the words of Jesus from Matthew 16:18: "I will build My church, and the gates of Hades shall not prevail against it." We think this verse gives us license to sit idly by as Jesus stands against hell's attacks for us. This passage, though it declares Christ's victory, does not in any way release us from active participation in the struggle against hell's intentions.

In God's covenant promise to Abraham He makes it clear that "your descendants shall possess the gate of their enemies" (Genesis 22:17). Part of our inherited blessings will be victory over the gates, the wicked councils and accusations of hell. One will never possess the gates of the enemy by compromise. If I expect my children to stand for what is right in their future then righteous living must begin with me in the present.

I said earlier in chapter 2 that if we leave out any one of the foundational principles that prepared Esther to write a decree to change the course of a nation, then we would never hold that same pen of authority in our hands. I said that the power of Esther's pen was not in the ink but in the character and resolve of the writer.

Beloved, this is one of those foundational principles that we cannot bypass. What would be the point of Esther writing a decree to reverse Haman's curse and accusation if she and her people have already fallen prey to Haman at the gate of the city? If they have already brokered a deal to live in peace and, in turn, reject their God-given purpose and destiny, then a decree would be unnecessary. It would make absolutely no sense for Esther to write anything. She would simply live out her life in the palace, all the while tolerating Haman and the paganism surrounding her.

If Mordecai had not stood for truth, there would not be a triumphant record of God's people reversing a curse. Esther would have remained an obscure queen that perhaps, with any luck, would have made it into the back pages of the Mede and Persian history. Ah, yes, there it is on page 5,346, section 4, paragraph 3, line 1a: "Esther, wife of King Ahasuerus." Her record would be tucked in somewhere between grain and oxen prices during the time of her husband's reign.

Perhaps the story of how she won the beauty contest and became queen of Persia might have followed oral tradition and been told for fifty years or so at bedtime to young Jewish girls, but after the fall of the Persian Empire her story would soon be forgotten. No, this one act of Mordecai to live for principle in the face of death turns a fairytale into a life-and-death drama that has inspired both Jews and Christians throughout history.

If Esther had submitted to the beauty process only to receive the favor of the king and a crown, there would not have been much significance to her life. But as we will see in our next chapter, Esther risked everything in order to preserve principle.

Do you want me to tell you the gut-wrenching reality of our generation? In our quest for more of the King's favor and blessing, we have forgotten the price Jesus paid on the cross for our sins. The pendulum has swung away from a crucified lifestyle, which calls us to hate sin and shun evil. I really think we are afraid that if we love the life of the cross and make a decision to live righteously that somehow we might fall into a legalistic trap and miss out on blessing and favor.

But it has never been either/or. It has always been both/and. I am called to both obedience and blessing; sacrifice and joy; suffering and prosperity; struggle and Kingdom glory. As we saw in chapter 1, it is the pain of the process that later on brings the triumphal procession. It was on the cross that Christ canceled the written code that stood opposed to us. How can anything less than the full appropriation of the cross in our lives reverse the adversary's accusations and release us to decree justice in Jesus' name? We will never gain that kind of resolve if we are hunched over at the gate of the enemy, bowing to our Hamans and living in the fallacy of the palace.

DELIVERANCE AND ENLARGEMENT

"For if you remain completely silent at this time [*enlargement*, KJV], and deliverance will arise for the Jews from another place, but you and your father's house will perish. Yet who knows whether you have come to the kingdom for such a time as this?"

Did you see it? This passage, Esther 4:14, holds one of the keys to Esther's favor. I have often missed it because I have misunderstood Mordecai's question. For years I used this question to drive home the importance of God's timing: "Who knows whether you have come to the kingdom for such a time as this?"

It has been a great biblical one-liner. I have used it again and again to challenge people about their gifts and callings. "See? It's time to step up to the plate and accept

God's call to reach your generation for Christ! Who knows whether or not you have come into the Kingdom for such a time as this?"

But then I read the passage again. And from a different perspective, I realized that Mordecai has taken hold of something much deeper and much more significant than a personal challenge to a young cousin. Even as he directs Esther to appear before the king and make an appeal on behalf of their people, Mordecai is looking beyond the present danger, for Esther will be taking a great risk by following his advice. In fact, she makes sure that he knows what he is asking:

> "All the king's servants and the people of the king's provinces know that any man or woman who goes into the inner court to the king, who has not been called, he has but one law: put all to death, except the one to whom the king holds out the golden scepter, that he may live. Yet I myself have not been called to go in to the king these thirty days."
>
> Esther 4:11

If she appears before the king without being summoned, the law reaches one verdict: death. She is reminding Mordecai that if the king does not wish to see her, she will not even get the chance to deliver a plea for her people. Yet Mordecai knows something about God's sovereign purpose and he expresses his understanding in two key words: *deliverance* and *enlargement*. Mordecai knows that God is interested not only in delivering Esther and the Jews from Haman's plot but also in enlarging the influence of His people Israel in order to fulfill the purpose of His Kingdom.

As we have seen in earlier chapters, the book of Esther is a Kingdom book. What does that mean again? Well, the Kingdom of God is the rule, reign and dominion of God in the earth. Jesus came preaching that the Kingdom of God (His rule) was at hand.

The people of Israel fulfilled God's Kingdom purpose in two significant ways. They preserved God's Word and commandments, and they became the nation that brought forth the Messiah, Jesus. This is why Esther is such a pivotal Kingdom book: Should God's people be annihilated, His promise of a deliverer through Abraham's seed cannot be fulfilled.

If Haman's plots are fulfilled, the seed of Abraham will be completely destroyed. Imagine that! The very promise of God for our salvation, given to us by generation after generation of prophets, is in the hands of one young Jewish woman.

I believe Mordecai knows well the words of those prophets, and that is why he is so direct with the queen. He knows that God's promise of One who will both deliver and enlarge is certain. Messianic prophecies are filled with declarations of deliverance and enlargement:

For unto us a Child is born, unto us a Son is given; and the government will be upon His shoulder. And His name will be called Wonderful, Counselor, Mighty God, Everlasting Father, Prince of Peace [deliverance]. Of the increase of His government and peace there will be no end [enlargement], upon the throne of David and over His kingdom, to order it and establish it with judgment and justice from that time forward, even forever. The zeal of the LORD of hosts will perform this.

Isaiah 9:6–7

And again:

> He shall have dominion also [deliverance] from sea to sea [enlargement], and from the River to the ends of the earth.
>
> Psalm 72:8

Shock Waves

That flutter you feel in your chest right now when you read the words of Isaiah and the psalmist and think of Esther and her king are God's way of reminding us: Nothing in Scripture is without purpose. God has been telling us the same story over and over again, so that someday it will seep inside us and we will open our eyes. The King wants to show His beautiful Bride to the world. That is why Mordecai's question must have sent a shock wave through Esther's heart, too: "Who knows whether you have come to the kingdom for such a time as this?"

If we see the question only in the context of time and timing, we miss its depth. The key word of the question is not *time* but *this*. "Who knows whether you have come to the kingdom for such a time as *this*?" Mordecai is doing more than giving a lecture on the joy of coming into the time when you know you are fulfilling a particular purpose or destiny. Rather, he is drawing attention to the particular moment he and Esther are facing. Great changes are about to take place. A great deliverance and enlargement is brewing in the heart of God, and He is ready to pour it out upon His people. The bride Esther has made herself ready and has come into the kingdom to ensure that the House of David will have no end.

Living in Esther's Time

I said earlier that the book of Esther is a prophetic book for a prophetic time. We, the Bride of Christ, are living in "Esther time": a time of great change just prior to a great deliverance. Scripture defines clearly the times we are approaching: "But know this, that in the last days perilous times will come" (2 Timothy 3:1).

Like Mordecai we must understand our time. The sons of Issachar "had understanding of the times, to know what Israel ought to do" (1 Chronicles 12:32) and so should we. Mordecai is confident that God will provide a way of escape because Israel's history has proven to him that God's grace to His people in times of peril always expresses itself in two ways: deliverance and enlargement.

I have good news for you. God is interested not only in delivering you from destruction but also in enlarging your borders and sphere of influence after the deliverance comes. Mordecai has hidden this truth deep within his heart. And we can see from Genesis to Revelation that in God's program, deliverance and enlargement go hand in hand.

Look at the life of Joseph. He is delivered out of the pit of death and sold as a slave to Potiphar. God expands his influence and he is placed in charge of everything Potiphar owns. Next he is delivered from the temptation of adultery with Potiphar's wife. And although he is accused falsely and thrown into prison, God enlarges his influence and he is placed in charge of the entire prison. Then God delivers Joseph from the prison and enlarges his influence once again: He is placed in charge of Pharaoh's palace and given rule over all the land of Egypt. Under his leadership Egypt prospers. Deliverance and enlargement!

71

But wait, it does not stop there. Because of Joseph's wisdom and discernment, God delivers Egypt from a terrible famine and Egypt becomes the breadbasket of the world. Joseph's influence is enlarged once again. This time he goes global.

Notice the progression: Delivered from a pit of death and enlarged to manage the household of a high-ranking official; delivered from temptation and enlarged to manage a large government penal institution; delivered from prison and enlarged to influence a king, a palace and a nation; delivered from famine and enlarged to influence the known world. Deliverance and enlargement!

Now how does Joseph explain it all? Does he see God's sovereign work of grace in this dual ministry of deliverance and enlargement? Resoundingly, yes. When he reveals his identity to his brothers, who have come down to Egypt to buy grain, here is how he explains the events of his life:

"And God sent me before you to preserve a posterity for you in the earth, and to save your lives by a great deliverance. So now it was not you who sent me here, but God; and He has made me a father to Pharaoh [enlargement], and lord of all his house [enlargement], and a ruler throughout all the land of Egypt [enlargement]."

Genesis 45:7–8

Shall I go on? Take the life of David. He is a shepherd boy whose influence extends to a few sheep in the hill country of Bethlehem. Yet because David trusts in God's faithful deliverance, he experiences enlargement throughout his life. Look at how it begins: David faces a lion and a bear in hand-to-hand combat and wins. As a result his influence

72

is enlarged and he faces a giant of a man. When King Saul asks David how on earth he thinks he can go up against Goliath, David's simple response is, "The LORD, who delivered me from the paw of the lion and from the paw of the bear, He will deliver me from the hand of this Philistine" (1 Samuel 17:37). Deliverance and enlargement!

In his lifetime David is delivered from a lion, a bear, a giant warrior, a jealous king and a son who betrays him. Each deliverance brings greater influence and enlargement. He becomes king over all of Israel and ultimately influences all of human history. Does David discern what God is doing? Does he see God's sovereign program of deliverance that leads to enlargement? Listen to the words of one of his psalms: "Hear me when I call, O God of my righteousness! You have [*enlarged*, KJV] me when I was in distress" (Psalm 4:1).

"You enlarged my path under me. . . . I have pursued my enemies and overtaken them" (Psalm 18:36–37).

Going Global

Mordecai has good reason to believe that deliverance and enlargement are on the Jewish horizon. He is drawing from a rich knowledge of God's sovereign work among His people. So what exactly is Mordecai saying to young Queen Esther? Here is the Aaron Früh paraphrase:

Esther, God has this ministry called deliverance and enlargement. It's already arising in our midst. God has proven Himself faithful in our history as a nation. Whenever we have been in great peril and cried out to Him, He has delivered us. But God does not want to stop there. His sovereign will is to expand our influence in the earth in order

73

to touch all the nations of the world through the Messiah who will one day come through our Jewish people.

Esther, don't be confused or troubled by our present situation. Yes, Haman is going postal but we are going global! God is going to deliver us from Haman and expand our influence throughout all the earth. Through our people, all the families of the earth will be blessed. God has proclaimed it.

You have a choice here. Who knows whether or not you have risen to royalty in the Persian kingdom in order to be a leader in God's deliverance and enlargement ministry? If you want in on the ground floor of the marvelous deliverance God is ready to perform, then there is no better time than now. If not, then we as a nation will move on to deliverance and enlargement through someone else, but your legacy will be lost.

When I look at the question Mordecai poses to Esther from this perspective I realize how often you and I miss the point of what God is trying to do through our trials. We conclude that the trial is here to stay. That our season of difficulty will continue and, in fact, grow worse. We remain silent even as the ceiling of oppression is lowered down upon us. I wonder how many saints who were called to great influence in critical times never did more than tend a few sheep because they were afraid of the lion and the bear? This is exactly what Mordecai is saying to Esther: "Listen to me. Haman's noose is tightening. It won't be easy, but you have position and influence that God can use to save us."

We all face a Haman. If we do not deal with him faithfully and courageously, he will never stop agitating us. Like the Energizer Bunny he keeps going and going.

Haman, in fact, is not just a random bad guy. You will recall that he is the son of Hammedatha the Agagite, a direct descendant of King Agag, the king of the Amalekites. Remember King Agag? God commanded King Saul to completely destroy King Agag and all the Amalekites because of their treatment of the Jews as they came out of Egypt (see 1 Samuel 15:2–3; see also Exodus 17:14). Saul only partially fulfills God's word to "utterly destroy" Amalek (1 Samuel 15:3). Instead of putting Agag to death, Saul spares him and misses his moment of deliverance.

Because he refuses to defeat Haman's ancestors, he never enlarges his influence. As a result of his appeasement regarding Agag, he loses his kingship. Samuel says to him, "The LORD has torn the kingdom of Israel from you" (1 Samuel 15:28).

Lesson: If you don't destroy your Hamans, they will destroy you. Saul fails to accept God's deliverance that leads to enlargement, and as a result Israel has had to confront the Amalekites for centuries.

And yet, as Mordecai indicated to Queen Esther, the Lord will provide a way of deliverance for His people. Consider how the hate-filled, murderous spirit of Haman continues to breathe out threats against Jewish people. Anti-Semitism, born in the hearts of the Amalekites, continues today in their descendants all over the world. But a quick glance at Israel's modern-day history, beginning with its war of independence in 1948, confirms that God's program of deliverance and enlargement is still in progress. Each time Israel has been attacked its army has been severely outnumbered and outgunned. Yet in each major war, not only has Israel been delivered but its landmass has been enlarged by thousands of square miles.

When Israel was established as a nation, it consisted of 3,000 square miles. After the war of independence in 1948, its borders more than doubled in size to 8,000 square miles. After the 1967 Six-Day War, Israel's land increased to 26,000 square miles, and after the 1973 Yom Kippur war it increased to 36,000 square miles. When the state of Israel was established a little more than fifty years ago there were fewer than one million people living in the land. Today there are six million. Deliverance and enlargement!

Temporary Trials

It is vital, as children of God, that we recognize that our trials are only temporary. Are you in a difficult season? Take heart. It is bound to change. You will not be stuck in a tough spot forever. Prepare now for the enlargement of your influence. Deliverance and enlargement are on the rise on your behalf. If you have fallen, you will rise again.

Maybe you are in Joseph's pit of despair. It is okay. We have all been there, done that and gotten the T-shirt. Start crawling up the sides if you have to. And as long as you are in there, don't live your life in the rearview mirror. You cannot change your past. Prepare now in today's pit for tomorrow's promotion. It is coming. You can be sure of it! Mordecai was.

Maybe you are facing the lion of temptation. Scripture teaches that Satan goes about like a roaring lion seeking out people to destroy. Maybe Potiphar's wife is trying to ruin your good testimony. Remember: If you will stay true to God when tested by the lion of temptation, your deliverance and promotion are sure to follow.

Maybe you are working for a boss who seems to embody the spirit of Saul. He belittles and attacks you constantly.

Filled with pride and jealousy, he has made you into a target. Take heart; this too shall pass. Continue to show respect and never pay back evil for evil. Perhaps he will soon be gone and you will have his position. Go out and buy a can of Lemon Pledge and some window cleaner. You are going to need them both when you move into your new corner office.

As a pastor I can tell you numerous stories of men and women who faced all kinds of circumstances just like these. Yet they continued to pray for those who were persecuting them. In time they were not only delivered but also enlarged and promoted. Oh, yes, they went through some rough waters. But in the midst of the storm they remained true to their faith and God honored them.

Perhaps, as happened to David of old, someone very close to you is betraying you. For David it was his son Absalom who tried to take the kingdom from him. I think that betrayal is the most difficult trial to bear. But you can take heart even in betrayal because God's deliverance and enlargement ministry works here as well. In fact there is a special blessing for those who are betrayed.

I find a common thread in the aftermath of betrayal: global influence. Joseph was betrayed by his brothers, yet his wisdom and discernment saved the known world from starvation. David was betrayed by his son, but the storm finally broke. His example of leadership, his passion for music and worship, and his plans for building God's Temple all have bearing on our lives thousands of years later. Judas betrayed Jesus and . . . need I say more? So if betrayal lies at your door, take heart; you will be amazed to see where God will take you.

Keep reading. You will see how Esther's influence was enlarged. Why? Because she was willing to accept her time of deliverance and face her enemy.

6

Please Remain Standing

My wife, Sharon, and I were pastors of a church in Chicago for eight years. Our apartment was located in a section on the near north side of Chicago affectionately known as "Wrigley Ville," home to Wrigley Field and the Chicago Cubs. We lived there in the days of Harry Carry and Jack Brickhouse, and before Wrigley Field followed the rest of the professional stadiums and added lights for night baseball games.

There is nothing quite like walking over to the historic field on a warm summer's day to watch the Cubbies, win or lose. It is not unusual for out-of-town business people to attend a Cubs game caring not in the least whom the Cubs are playing. They just want to witness America's game played in one of the only fields left from the era when baseball was our national pastime.

At Wrigley you don't need binoculars to see the players. For a snack, you down a Chicago dog hugged by a poppy seed bun, smothered with lettuce, tomato and onions and, if you are really brave, green peppers. You would never dream of dining on sushi or sprouts as they do in the more sophisticated ballparks.

I have been to Wrigley Field on cold days in the spring and fall and seen faithful Cubbies fans buttoned down in their parkas under plaid blankets with teeth chattering. The weather was more suited for ice fishing than watching baseball.

Yet when Jack Brickhouse said "Please remain standing" as he introduced the performer who would lead us in the National Anthem, those Cubs fans, true to form, shed their warmers and their hats, placed their hands over their hearts and bellowed out the anthem—shivering between every word. Cold, but faithfully standing.

Many times these fans were cheering for the team that was last place in their division. Beaten, but faithfully standing.

In the seventh-inning stretch in those days, when Harry Carry stood up and opened the window of the press box, you knew that it was time to stand with him. "Everyone standing," his distinct voice would shudder. "Everyone on your feet!" When Harry stood up no one dared to stay seated in the bleachers. At that moment it mattered not whether you were a Cubs fan, a Padres fan, a Braves fan or a Cardinals fan. All that mattered was that we all loved baseball. We were all Americans under a clear blue summer sky standing up with Harry as he led us from the press box in a rousing chorus of "Take Me Out to the Ballgame!"

We had all, for a moment, slipped back into America the way she used to be. In a sense we were standing and cheering for the things that represent the things we love—the American flag, hot dogs, apple pie, Chevrolets and old-time baseball. "Buy me some peanuts and crackerjacks . . . at the old ballgame."

There is no argument in baseball lore that Cubbies fans are the most loyal to their team. (Well, okay, this could be open for debate.) Whether they remain standing for the National Anthem or remain standing for the seventh-inning stretch, Cubs fans remain faithful, win or lose.

The Final Innings

Now you are probably wondering what the Chicago Cubs and the book of Esther have in common. First a quick review of what we know about this amazing story so far.

King Ahasuerus desires to display the beauty of his bride on the seventh day of the feast. As we saw earlier, seven is the number of perfection and completion. Prophetically we are living in the seventh day—a day when Christ is perfecting the beauty of His Church.

I have heard Bible prophecy teachers say that on the prophetic time clock, we are at five minutes to midnight. It is time for the Church to trim her lamps and fill them with fresh oil as we await the Bridegroom's appearance.

If you would indulge me for a moment, though, I would like to paint this picture in a slightly different hue. Maybe, in a strange and surreal way, the Church is in the seventh-inning stretch . . . in a place like Wrigley Field. Because at Wrigley it is not the color of the uniform that matters, it is the fact that we love baseball. And at this point, in the last days, it matters not whether we are Presbyterian fans, Baptist fans, Methodist fans, charismatic-Pentecostal fans. . . .

81

What matters is that we are all Christians standing together in agreement, singing the song of the redeemed and standing faithfully for the things we love most: Jesus Christ and Him crucified, His life and teachings, His resurrection from the dead and our faith in His name.

However you best illustrate and portray it, what is at issue here is that the Church is called to stand faithfully in unity during this final moment of time.

At this juncture of our journey through the book of Esther, Mordecai has appealed to the queen to stand before the king and ask him to overturn his ruling to annihilate the Jews. With Mordecai's grim reminder that she will certainly perish if she does not act and his encouragement that God intends to bring about great deliverance for His people, Esther agrees. She tells Mordecai to join all the Jews of the capital city together to stand with her in agreement for three days of fasting before she goes before the king.

Chapter 5 of Esther opens with these words:

> Now it happened on the third day that Esther put on her royal robes and stood in the inner court of the king's palace, across from the king's house, while the king sat on his royal throne in the royal house, facing the entrance of the house. So it was, when the king saw Queen Esther *standing* in the court, that she found favor in his sight, and the king held out to Esther the golden scepter that was in his hand. Then Esther went near and touched the top of the scepter. And the king said to her, "What do you wish, Queen Esther? What is your request? It shall be given to you—up to half my kingdom!"
>
> Esther 5:1–3, emphasis added

It is the exact moment when the king sees Esther standing in the court that she receives his favor. Do you see any connection? What brings the incredible favor of the king? What causes him to hold out the golden scepter to Esther and grant half of his kingdom to her?

The King's Favor

Actually we have already discovered in the first four chapters of the book of Esther what unleashes this incredible flow of favor in chapter 5. Esther has focused on the process of becoming beautiful. She is faithful to the regulations for beautification even though they include six months of bitter myrrh. She gains God's royal crown of endurance long before she wears the queenly crown. Esther not only walks in two-dimensional obedience to God and man but also trusts in God's "deliverance and enlargement" program. Finally she joins in fasting with all of the Jews of her city for three days and three nights.

We need to be careful lest we take the king's response to be one of favoritism. It is not favoritism that Esther experiences when she stands before the king; it is favor born in the heart of God the Father and expressed through the scepter in the outstretched arm of a pagan king.

Any road to this kind of favor will have the same stops along the way. You cannot stop at Elim until you have stopped at Marah. You cannot stand before the king in royal apparel wearing the crown of endurance until you have endured.

Your victory will be much sweeter if you remain standing when you are at the bottom of your game and when everyone seems to be on a winning streak but you. When your myrrh moment feels as though it is turning into one of those long myrrh seasons, please remain standing.

As we saw in the fourth chapter of Esther, Haman's initial anger against the Jews starts because Mordecai remains standing in his presence, refusing to bow as he passes through the king's gate. The king's servants ask Mordecai daily why he does not honor Haman but he does not answer them. Look at the King James Version's rendering of Esther 3:4, a verse we observed earlier:

> Now it came to pass, when they spake daily unto him, and he hearkened not unto them, that they told Haman, to see whether Mordecai's matters would stand: for he had told them that he was a Jew.

Excuse me for the play on words, but does it really "matter" if someone stands up for his or her convictions? We can see that it matters a great deal to the Jewish people of Haman's day. Haman devises his wicked plan to annihilate the Jews all because one man, Mordecai, takes a stand on a matter he truly believes in. As a Jew he cannot bow in homage or give reverence to anyone but God. So, in consequence, all of the Jews join in a fast and Esther risks her life to stand before the king in order to save her people from a holocaust. All because one man, Mordecai, will not bow before a false god. He remains *standing!*

However you slice it, there are a lot of people faithfully standing in the book of Esther. One theme running through the whole book that we will discover again is the power of standing in agreement. It is displayed beautifully in the warm relationship between Esther and her cousin Mordecai and their willingness to stand together for a righteous cause. And twice we read of the Jews that they gathered together in unity to stand for their lives (see Esther 8:11; 9:16, KJV).

In this "seventh day," this day of completion, we believers are likewise called to gather together in unity to stand for Christ and His Kingdom.

Standing Together

Woven in between the lines of the book of Esther is the unspoken understanding that Mordecai and Esther see themselves as representatives of God's chosen people dating back to the patriarchs. In our last chapter we saw how Mordecai reminds Esther of God's historic deliverance and enlargement program throughout the ages. Mordecai warns Esther that if she will not stand with him for the Jews, she, as well as her father's name, will perish at the hands of their enemies. He means that her father's name (though he was already dead) and her father's line of descent would be erased.

Standing before the king, then, Esther represents not only the Jews in Persia but also the legacy of her forefathers, the covenants, the commandments, the Davidic kingly line and the Messianic promises attached to it.

Just as Esther stands as a representative, united with the present Jews but also connected with the patriarchs and promises, so, too, do we. We stand as representative characters of not only the Old Testament saints but also the early Church and the followers of Jesus throughout Christian history. Hebrews 12:1 explains that today we are "surrounded by so great a cloud of witnesses." They are presently cheering us on from the bleachers in heaven and hoping that we carry on in the tradition of their favorite pastime: endurance running.

> Therefore we also, since we are surrounded by so great a
> cloud of witnesses, let us lay aside every weight, and the

sin which so easily ensnares us, and let us run with endurance the race that is set before us, looking unto Jesus, the author and finisher of our faith.

Hebrews 12:1–2

The writer of Hebrews connects the saints under the Old Covenant with the saints under the new and makes it clear that the Old Testament saints cannot cross the finish line if we, the saints of the final generation, fail to stand together in unity and keep the tradition of our faith alive and vibrant. Hebrews 11:39–40 says, "And all these, having obtained a good testimony through faith, did not receive the promise, God having provided something better for us, that they should not be made perfect apart from us." Notice the words *they should not be made perfect apart from us*. That is huge. Every time you and I stand in unity with our brothers and sisters in Christ, be it in a worship service, a common Kingdom purpose or just working out the conflicts in everyday relationships, we are standing as representatives of the saints of old. As we get closer to the finish line, so do they.

The Christian life is not a fifty-yard dash, nor is it a marathon; it is a relay race. Every generation has the responsibility to carry the torch, stand for the things of Christ and pass the torch on to the coming generation.

If we are the final runners in the race, then we should be aware of the awesome responsibility of carrying this age-old torch—and of our responsibility to the Kingdom and the past, present and future that it represents. Part of our becoming "glorious" depends on this truth. It is when the king sees Esther standing that he shows her his favor.

Walk in Love and Unity

Beloved, could it be that the true beauty of Christian character comes from a willingness to stand with other believers in a spirit of unity? Paul makes it clear in Ephesians 4:13 that we can never receive the full measure of Christ "till we all come to the unity of the faith." In other words we cannot walk in fullness until we walk in love.

The same is clear in 1 Corinthians 1:10:

Now I plead with you, brethren, by the name of our Lord Jesus Christ, that you all speak the same thing, and that there be no divisions among you, but that you be perfectly joined together in the same mind and in the same judgment.

And also in 2 Corinthians 13:11:

Finally, brethren, farewell. Become complete. Be of good comfort, be of one mind, live in peace; and the God of love and peace will be with you.

Want favor? Take a stand for unity.

I believe in team ministry, especially through the expression of the priesthood family. Sharon and I and our four children work together in the ministry. We form a partnership that is committed first to Christ, then to each other and then to the Body of Christ.

The other pastors of our congregation have formed the same priesthood family partnerships. The spouses of our pastors are employed at the church in different capacities of pastoral ministry. Husbands and wives work together in their respective callings and neither is threatened by the other's anointing. In each case the wife's

87

gifts are strong where her husband's are weak, and her husband's are strong where hers are weak. Sharon, for example, is excellent in administration and planning. That is my greatest weakness. As a team we complement one another.

I remember a Sunday two years ago when we were planning to baptize a number of new believers. The church was alive with praise, and I was up front, worshiping God, as one of our pastors led the singing. Another pastor and the first baptism candidate were preparing to step into the waters of the baptismal tank, when the looks on their faces showed that something was terribly wrong. Instead of stepping into gently warmed water, they were about to plunge into a volcano. Something had gone wrong with the thermostat; you could have had a crab boil up there that morning. But you know what? I never noticed. I was worshiping God, captivated by His majesty. Who took matters into her own hands and led a team of ice carriers to the baptismal? You guessed it: my wife, the one who excels in administration and planning. Boy, were they happy to see Sharon with the ice brigade!

If my family is not walking in unity and if our pastors and leaders are not walking and living in unity, how can we expect the Church corporately to stand in unity in the inner court of God's presence and experience His favor?

I love what David says in Psalm 133:1–3:

Behold, how good and how pleasant it is for brethren to dwell together in unity! It is like the precious oil upon the head, running down on the beard, the beard of Aaron, running down on the edge of his garments. It is like the dew of Hermon, descending upon the mountains of Zion; for there the LORD commanded the blessing—life forevermore.

You see, unity and blessing go hand in hand. The Scriptures call us to walk in unity in the midst of diversity. Romans 12:5 says: "So we, being many, are one body in Christ, and individually members of one another." Until we get a handle on this truth and begin to practice it, our beauty will merely be skin deep. The Lord will never "command His blessing" upon our lives. Had Esther, Mordecai and the Jews been divided and not seen themselves as representatives of all who would come after them, Esther would not have stood before the king in all of her beauty requesting protection for the Jews.

Think of how many churches miss the opportunity to reach their communities because they will not stand together in agreement. They allow strife to destroy the unity that comes from the bond of peace. The words of James are sobering: "For where envy and self-seeking exist, confusion and every evil thing will be there" (James 3:16).

Think of how many Christian homes are filled with ugly disharmony because of an unwillingness to stand together in love.

And tell me, why is it that the most segregated place in America is the church on Sunday mornings? Such things ought not to be. And the Bible calls us to go even further than integration. It calls us to reconciliation.

In all of these issues the saying is true: "United we stand and divided we fall." This does not mean, of course, that we are willing to trade sound doctrine for the sake of unity. That price would be too high. But finding common ground within the basic fundamentals of our faith in Christ allows lots of room for relationship building outside of our particular corner of truth.

The Promise Keepers movement is a wonderful example of this. One of the most enriching experiences of my life was to stand in the Georgia Dome in Atlanta with fifty thousand pastors from around the world in the largest gathering of pastors in the history of the Church. Witnessing leaders at this pastors' conference from the Four Square movement, Free Church, Southern Baptist and Assemblies of God, among many others, all lifting up Christ together was just a taste of what is before us.

Erasing Our Differences

I believe that in this seventh-inning stretch, denominational, doctrinal and relational schisms will be purged from the Church of the living Lord. There will still be plenty of diversity in our expressions of worship, but the difference will simply be that we will not fight about our differences any longer.

This does not negate the fact that a false church will continue to rise and increasingly reject the faith of the Gospel. But the true Church will grow stronger and more vibrant and persecution will knit the members of the Bride together as one, erasing the demarcation of age-old denominational and racial barriers.

It is happening already. The lifting of hands used to be practiced only by charismatics and Pentecostals. Today we find people of many denominations lifting their hands in adoration of Jesus. And look at music. It used to be that contemporary worship songs were only sung in certain churches. Now, true to what Jesus is doing in perfecting His Bride and making her of one mind, it is rare that a church does not sing at least a few choruses.

Recently I was riding in the car with our college-and-career pastor, Scott Jacobsen Moore, when he said, "You've got to hear this new song." He started the CD and, to my amazement, I heard the words, "Heaven came down and glory filled my soul, when at the cross the Savior made me whole." When I began to sing along Scott was impressed. "Wow!" he said. "You must like this artist as much as I do." He could not believe it when I told him that the song was actually a decades-old hymn and that I had grown up singing it. What blessed me about it was that young artists are seeing the value of the hymns and the truth that each song spoke to its generation.

And this is not true just with the style of music that we enjoy. In each generation since the Middle Ages, God has restored to His Church truths and ministries that were lost during that era. Evangelism, healing, worship, teaching, mission work. Peter encouraged his hearers to be "established in the present truth" (2 Peter 1:12).

To embrace only what God is doing in our generation is to live a disjointed Christianity. We stand as a representation of all of the truth God has restored to the Body of Christ throughout the life of the Church.

In Esther's time the Jews gather to stand together and she then stands before the king. The Scripture teaches, "Unto him shall the gathering of the people be" (Genesis 49:10, KJV). As we gather together in the inner court of His presence in one accord, standing boldly before God, bathed in myrrh, wrinkle-free, walking in complete obedience and enjoying the favor of all the people, we stand not alone. We are standing with the corporate Body of Christian believers both past and present and with the patriarchs of old, all desiring His Kingdom to come and His will to be done.

God cannot help but command His blessing upon us if we have chosen to stand in unity. May we, therefore, please remain standing!

How to Make a Godly Appeal

W hat I am about to share with you is a life principle that I have practiced for thirty years. As a
result of living out this simple principle in my
daily walk with God, I am learning how to enjoy both the
favor of God and the favor of man.

There have been many times in my life when I found
myself in a quandary only to emerge unscathed. Since I
started practicing this principle as a young teenager I have
learned that experiencing both the favor of God and the
favor of man is not based on personal charisma or special
ability. These are simply rewards for practicing the biblical
principle of making a godly appeal.

I grew up in a single-parent home. My father was on his
way to church on the night before Christmas Eve when a
drunk driver killed him. I was only three years old. When I

was nine I went door to door in our neighborhood appealing for odd jobs—mowing lawns, pulling weeds, whatever I could get. I landed my first job with an elderly woman who owned an insurance company. Soon I was mowing her lawn and pulling weeds at her office.

At thirteen I got a job washing dishes in a restaurant. Soon I was promoted to bussing tables and one year later promoted to short-order cook. At seventeen I was the head cook.

I left the restaurant business and started bagging groceries in a large grocery chain; the benefits were better. After one year of hustling carts I was promoted to clerk and a few years later, at the age of 21, I was the night closing manager. I paid my way through Bible college on the salary from that job and saved enough to enter a seminary in Chicago.

When you have no father you learn quickly that faithfulness to God and faithfulness to an employer are ingredients for promotion. When openings arose I made an appeal to those in authority, promising that I could handle the responsibility. Most of the time I was too young and inexperienced but they listened to my appeal and gave me a chance.

Of all of the people in Scripture who practice this principle, Esther stands out as my favorite. Esther turns the tide of evil back toward the enemy because she makes an appeal to King Ahasuerus for the lives of her fellow Jews living in Persia.

Our law in this country allows a defendant who has been found guilty by one judge to appeal to a higher court. This is exactly what Esther does when Haman secures a horrible judgment against the Jews: She appeals to a higher power.

It must have been a terrifying moment when the Jews in the land heard what had happened. Remember Haman's words:

> "Let a decree be written that they [the Jewish nation] be destroyed." . . . And the king said to Haman, "The money and the people are given to you, to do with them as seems good to you." . . . And the letters were sent by couriers into all the king's provinces, to destroy, to kill, and to annihilate all the Jews, both young and old, little children and women, in one day, on the thirteenth day of the twelfth month . . . and to plunder their possessions. A copy of the document was to be issued as law in every province, being published for all people, that they should be ready for that day.
>
> Esther 3:9, 11, 13–14

As we have seen, Esther has every right to fear what might happen to her by appearing unannounced before the king. Still she agrees to take that chance so that she might appeal to this earthly king to waive the written judgment. But first she appeals in intercession to the highest court, to the most just Judge. For three days, before she pleads her case before King Ahasuerus, she and all her maids and servants appeal to the Most High God in His courtroom.

There is a divine principle here. Because Esther intercedes in the heavenly courthouse, God intercedes in the earthly one. Before we appeal to our earthly authorities we should always appeal to our heavenly one.

You see, God has placed strategically in and over our lives various people who can show us favor and grant us promotion. But before we stand in their presence with a request for favor we must first stand in God's presence. In His presence I am matured, prepared and given instructions on making my appeal a viable one.

Patient Preparation

Many people fail at making an appeal because they lack maturity and patient preparation. They fail to make their requests known to God first so that His peace can guard their hearts from irritation and frustration when it is time to go before the one they must petition.

Imagine if Esther had gone in to the king abruptly and demanded justice for her people. Would she have been justified in doing so? Certainly. A great injustice was about to occur and the king was not aware of the true implications of his written judgment. But, though her cause was just, if she had acted in that way, both she and her cousin would have been hanged on the gallows.

You see we sometimes sacrifice preparation because we want to right a wrong as quickly as possible. The Bible says, "For exaltation comes neither from the east nor from the west nor from the south. But God is the Judge: He puts down one, and exalts another" (Psalm 75:6–7). When Job faced his troubles he said, "Though He slay me, yet will I trust Him. Even so, I will defend my own ways before Him. . . . See now, I have prepared my case, I know that I shall be vindicated" (Job 13:15, 18). David prayed, "Hear a just cause, O Lord, . . . give ear to my prayer that is not from deceitful lips. Let my vindication come from Your presence; let Your eyes look on the things that are upright" (Psalm 17:1–2).

If you appeal to the highest court in prayer, your day in the earthly court of men will come and you will be vindicated.

Your vindication may take a while but things will be set in order. A quick glance again at Joseph's life will assure you of that. Joseph was sold into slavery by his own brothers and later accused falsely by Potiphar's wife and thrown into prison. After twenty years of injustice he was promoted from the dungeon to the palace in one day! Later he saw his plight as part of God's master timetable. He told his brothers, "You meant this for evil but God meant it for good, for the saving of many people." Though Joseph was in an earthly prison he actually had been in God's preparatory school for greatness. Joseph waited patiently for his moment and when it came, his heart was not bitter or tainted with anxiety. As a result, he was propelled into a place of international prominence in one day. God's timing is indeed everything.

It is sad that many good Christians never experience vindication or promotion because they are afraid to make an appeal. They are afraid to ask. Asking is our right and our responsibility. Jesus said, "Ask, and it will be given to you" (Matthew 7:7). And God spoke these words through the psalmist: "Ask of Me, and I will give You the nations for Your inheritance, and the ends of the earth for Your possession" (Psalm 2:8).

Asking is oftentimes mistaken for begging. David said in Psalm 37:25, "I have not seen the righteous forsaken, nor his descendants begging bread." Righteous people are never called to beg but they are called consistently to ask.

You see, as a Christian I believe that God desires to transfer the earth's resources into righteous hands. What He needs to make the transaction complete are righteous people who are not afraid to make godly appeals.

We learned in our last chapter that when King Ahasuerus saw Esther standing in the inner court she found favor in his sight. She was not standing alone, but in the bond of agreement with her cousin Mordecai and with all of the Jews in the capital city of Shushan. This is a perfect preamble for her assignment: to plead for her people.

If we look back one step further we see that her assignment came to her because Mordecai, first and foremost, began seeking God's favor. When he learned of the king's decree, he put on sackcloth and ashes and "cried out with a loud and bitter cry" (Esther 4:1) at the king's gate. In every province, in fact, there was "great mourning among the Jews, with fasting, weeping, and wailing" (Esther 4:3) such that Esther sent one of the king's eunuchs, Hathach, to check out all the commotion. The time that Mordecai and his fellow Jews had spent petitioning heaven resulted in clear direction for the queen:

> Mordecai told [Hathach] all that had happened. . . . He also gave him a copy of the written decree for their destruction, which was given at Shushan, that he might show it to Esther and explain it to her, and that he might command her to go in to the king to make supplication to him and plead before him for her people.
>
> Esther 4:7–8

In modern terms Mordecai was asking Queen Esther to appeal the guilty verdict and death sentence against the Jews. We have all heard of death row inmates who appeal their sentences, hoping to gain a stay or reversal of the ticket to the electric chair.

As I examine Esther's landmark appeal to King Ahasuerus, I find four key principles that are essential in making a successful appeal. Esther has the right appearance, the right spirit, the right timing and the right approach.

The Right Appearance

First, Esther has the right appearance.

> Now it happened on the third day [of her fast] that Esther put on her royal robes and stood in the inner court of

98

the king's palace, across from the king's house, while the king sat on his royal throne in the royal house, facing the entrance of the house.

Esther 5:1

You may have a just cause as you approach your moment of appeal, but a misstep out of protocol may cost you some favor. I know people who have missed a promotion because, when it came time for their annual review, they were not dressed appropriately. Remember, God looks at your heart but man looks at your outward appearance, and if you want favor with God and man then you must not only have a pure heart but also be wearing the right stuff.

When Pharaoh called Joseph out of prison, did he leap up and run into the king's chamber? No.

Then Pharaoh sent and called Joseph, and they brought him hastily out of the dungeon; and he shaved, changed his clothing, and came to Pharaoh.

Genesis 41:14

So before you stand in the court of the king, remove every barrier to your plea and dress as the king expects you to dress. For Esther it meant one year of beauty preparations and her royal apparel. She gets it right and wins the right to speak.

The Right Spirit

Next, Esther has the right spirit. Notice Esther's communication with the king, revealing a teachable, humble spirit:

So Esther answered, "If it pleases the king . . ." (Esther 5:4).

"If I have found favor in the sight of the king, and if it pleases the king to grant my petition and fulfill my request . . ." (Esther 5:8).

"I will do as the king has said" (Esther 5:8).

Esther is one smart cookie. She is a queen on a mission from God and could easily come across as self-righteous and arrogant because of the heavy burden she carries to save her people from annihilation. But she also knows what happened to the last queen who stood her ground!

Ahasuerus is a powerful king in a man's world and telling him how to run his kingdom and change his decrees will be met with resistance or worse. Esther understands the cultural milieus of her day and makes her appeal accordingly.

This is a sound principle today. People in authority, be they male or female, do not appreciate being told how to handle their business.

This biblical principle of having a right spirit in order to make an appeal seems largely to have been lost in the attempt by many Christians to influence the culture of our day. We picket, point fingers and generally come across as mean-spirited people looking for a good street brawl. We not only make the politician into our adversary, we also alienate nonbelievers.

There is a new day dawning, however. Many "Esther" believers are working behind the scenes "under the radar" so to speak for biblical causes. They are appealing quietly through political and judicial channels to challenge anti-biblical movements and change the laws of our land, and they are succeeding.

You may have heard of the American Center for Law and Justice, for instance, just one such organization. Jay Sekulow, his law partner, Stuart J. Roth, and a team of lawyers represent Christian causes and issues across our nation. Jay has stood before the United States Supreme Court in Washington, D.C., more than any other lawyer of his age in the history of the court. These men and women are not out to light the fires of a Christian cultural revolution. They work quietly and steadily, and they and their appeals are bringing godliness into many areas of the government.

When approaching your moment of appeal be sure to have an attitude check. Your cause may be just, but if there is one slight hint of "righteous wrath" or indignation in you, you might lose your appeal. Your rejection will be based solely on your bad attitude, not on the merit of your cause. Instead of an audience with the judge, we often are held in contempt of court because of a contemptuous spirit. Esther's appeal is heard because she has a right spirit.

The Right Timing

Next, Esther has the right timing. Esther has on the right robes, the right makeup and the right spirit, but, as we have seen, her very presence in the inner court without an invitation from the king is against the law. Since Esther could very well be put to death without ever opening her mouth, timing is everything.

Sometimes when we believe that we have been accused falsely or wronged in some way, we are so intent on righting the wrong that we make our appeals abruptly without allowing God to work on our behalf. Give the Lord time to soften the heart of the person you are appealing to. Even when Esther gains audience with the king she does not unload her burden. She invites Ahasuerus and Haman to a luncheon that is already prepared.

101

So it was, when the king saw Queen Esther standing in the court, that she found favor in his sight, and the king held out to Esther the golden scepter that was in his hand. Then Esther went near and touched the top of the scepter. And the king said to her, "What do you wish, Queen Esther? What is your request? It shall be given to you—up to half my kingdom!" So Esther answered, "If it pleases the king, let the king and Haman come today to the banquet I have prepared for him." Then the king said, "Bring Haman quickly, that he may do as Esther has said." So the king and Haman went to the banquet that Esther had prepared.

Esther 5:2–5

Notice that Haman has to be called quickly because it is lunchtime. Esther goes to the king when his stomach is growling and says, "Dear, I've prepared a beautiful banquet of choice food and wine for you and Haman." What timing!

At the luncheon the king inquires for the second time what Esther's petition and request of him is, and he makes the same offer of up to half of the kingdom. At that moment Esther could express her deep concern and expose Haman for the evil man that he is, but again she waits. Here is her response to the king's second inquiry:

Then Esther answered and said, "My petition and request is this: If I have found favor in the sight of the king, and if it pleases the king to grant my petition and fulfill my request, then let the king and Haman come to the banquet which I will prepare for them, and tomorrow I will do as the king has said."

Esther 5:7–8

Wise Esther is carefully laying the groundwork for the appeal by subtly letting the king know that her desire is no small matter to her and that she needs the proper setting and the perfect time to express it.

Listen, your vindication will come but you need to give the Lord time to work on your behalf. This happens in Esther's situation. Because she waits for the proper timing, remarkable developments take place between the two banquets, a mere 24 hours apart.

First of all, Haman is elated that the queen invited him to a banquet of honor. He goes home and calls his wife, Zeresh, and his friends. He tells them of his great riches and his promotion and advancement above all of the other officials in the kingdom. Then he tells them of the queen's invitation. Suddenly, a saddened look falls upon Haman's countenance as he says,

> "Yet all this avails me nothing, so long as I see Mordecai the Jew sitting at the king's gate." Then his wife Zeresh and all his friends said to him, "Let a gallows be made, fifty cubits high, and in the morning suggest to the king that Mordecai be hanged on it; then go merrily with the king to the banquet." And the thing pleased Haman; so he had the gallows made.
>
> Esther 5:13–14

Because Esther waits, Haman's pride is setting him up for his own destruction. Chapter 6 opens with the king suffering from insomnia on the night before the second banquet that Esther is preparing. What do you do when you cannot sleep in the middle of an Arabian desert night in ancient times? Watch the History Channel! Ahasuerus calls his servants, and they bring in the record books that chronicle the history of his rule and reign, and they read him bedtime stories.

An interesting discovery is made as his servants are droning on through the night, reading column after column of the detailed records:

And it was found written that Mordecai had told of Bigthana and Teresh, two of the king's eunuchs, the doorkeepers who had sought to lay hands on King Ahasuerus.

Esther 6:2

Incredibly, the king's servants uncover the forgotten fact that Mordecai had uncovered a plot to assassinate the king. The king inquires about what honor has been given to Mordecai for saving his life and his servants tell him that nothing has been done.

Do you see how the hand of the Lord can work in the appeal process if we will weigh our timing carefully? Do you think it is any coincidence that Ahasuerus cannot sleep? Do you think that it is just happenstance that the discovery of Mordecai's good deed is made the night before Esther makes her appeal? Then at the very moment that the king is planning to bestow some kind of honor upon Mordecai, Haman arrives in the outer court to ask that Mordecai be hanged on the gallows!

He never gets the chance. Soon the king is giving him orders to parade Mordecai on the king's horse and in the king's robe in the city streets as one honored by the king: "The king said to Haman, 'Hasten, take the robe and the horse . . . and do so for Mordecai the Jew who sits within the king's gate'" (Esther 6:10).

There are three words in that verse that pave the way for Esther's appeal: *Mordecai the Jew*. If Esther had not waited the king would not have had this sudden appreciation for the Jews. Can you see how waiting even a few hours can pave the way for your appeal?

The Right Approach

Finally, Esther takes the right approach. Now, timing in place, Esther is ready for her appeal. At the second banquet she has prepared, King Ahasuerus asks again, a third time, "What is your petition and what is your request?" I think that by this time the king is more than curious. Here is Esther's appeal:

> Then Queen Esther answered and said, "If I have found favor in your sight, O king, and if it pleases the king, let my life be given me at my petition, and my people at my request. For we have been sold, my people and I, to be destroyed, to be killed, and to be annihilated. Had we been sold as male and female slaves, I would have held my tongue, although the enemy could never compensate for the king's loss." Then King Ahasuerus answered and said to Queen Esther, "Who is he, and where is he, who would dare presume in his heart to do such a thing?" And Esther said, "The adversary and enemy is this wicked Haman!" So Haman was terrified before the king and queen.
>
> Esther 7:3–6

Can you imagine the size of the lump in Haman's throat at that moment? I think he probably starts choking on the stuffed grape leaves and humus! What do you think his first thought is? Maybe, *I didn't know the queen was Jewish!* Or perhaps, *Oops, I built those gallows just a little too high.*

I love Esther's dual approach. She knows that the king has a business mind and wants to run a kingdom and have a little left for retirement. So she says, "Listen, king, from a business perspective you're going to incur a huge financial loss with this ethnic-cleansing proposal. The one who came up with this scheme will never compensate for the king's financial loss." She is saying that if the Jews are put to death, the kingdom will lose all the revenue that these industrious people are bringing into the treasury.

She also lets the king know that someone very near to him will perish in the evil plan as well. She is not vague on this point:

"Let my life be given me at my petition."
"For we have been sold, my people and I, to be destroyed, to be killed, and to be annihilated."

Esther is letting the king know that he will be affected personally in the loss of his wife and in the loss of revenue. Esther shows us that in making a godly appeal, it is usually wise to let the individual know the ultimate effect of his or her choice.

This reminds me how during World War II the quality control department of a parachute factory appealed to the female workers. The women were encouraged to take the utmost care in sewing the chutes because it could be their fathers, husbands, brothers or sons who would be depending on their craftsmanship as they jumped out of airplanes. The management was very wise in letting the workers know that their attention to detail might ultimately affect them.

Having the right appearance, the right spirit, the right timing and the right approach will make a world of difference in a godly appeal.

It did for me in the following situation.

Lunch with the Mayor

A few years ago here in Mobile, Alabama, our mayor was looking closely at casino gambling as a way to increase city revenues and fund education reform. The city budget was tight and Mobile was losing millions of dollars a year to the Mississippi Gulf Coast Casinos just a few miles away. The mayor surmised that if Mobile built casinos along the riverfront leading into Mobile Bay, we could improve public education as well as city services. A gambling referendum was placed before the voters and it passed with a 70 percent landslide victory for gambling. It was now up to the mayor and the city council to move forward with the gambling plan or come up with another way to cover the rising costs of running a city.

Mayor Mike Dow was now in a political pickle. On one side, the Christian community was lighting a firestorm against him and his reelection campaign, and, on the other side, 70 percent of the community were pushing the gambling option. There were petitions and vocal opposition circulating from both sides.

I was against gambling, but I knew that pointing a judgmental finger at the mayor would never give me an opportunity to make a godly appeal. Stuart J. Roth, an attorney whom I mentioned earlier, a dear friend, was a resident of Mobile at that time. We shared the sentiment that an "Esther" appeal to the mayor could bring us further along than joining the petition campaign.

We followed protocol and called the mayor's secretary asking for a lunch meeting. The mayor graciously accepted and a few weeks later we met him in a downtown restaurant.

Stuart and I had already laid the groundwork for the appeal and had decided beforehand that in this initial meeting we would not "spill" our concerns. Instead we asked the mayor about his concerns and the challenges he faced every day in leading the city. At the end of the meeting he inquired, "I suppose you gentlemen are here to talk to me about the gambling issue, right?"

"Actually," we answered, "we know that you are under a lot of heat right now and we wanted to treat you to lunch so that we could get to know you and ask you how we might best pray for your family."

Talk about a startled look! The mayor instantly let down his defenses and for the next half-hour shared with us personal prayer needs and issues he was facing in life. The restaurant emptied and we were still talking. Finally, at the end of the conversation, we prayed with the mayor for the needs he had expressed to us. When he opened his eyes, the mayor said, "No one has ever asked me how he could pray for me."

Wow! If nothing else happened that day, Stuart and I had just built a lifelong bond with a human being who just happened to be the mayor of our city. As we were leaving the restaurant the mayor asked us to meet again the following week to get our opinion on the gambling issue. God's timing at work.

Now the groundwork was in place. We shared mutual trust and a common concern for the same city. In our second "banquet" we assured the mayor that we understood that he had a genuine burden to fund education and that gambling seemed to be his only option. He discussed with us the different options that he had to increase revenue and we began to understand from his perspective why few of them were very viable. By the end of the lunch it seemed to us that his decision was cast in stone to go forward with the gambling issue. Besides, to back out now might very well be political suicide for him after the 70 percent referendum vote in favor of gambling.

As we concluded our conversation, Stuart and I presented our appeal. "Mayor Dow, we just want you to ask one question of yourself as you lay your head on your pillow tonight: How will gambling affect your family in five years?" It was an honest, sincere question on our part that appealed to the mayor's good sense. He knew that we were not being judgmental or condemning but were, like him, concerned for the future of his family.

Basically, as with Esther's appeal, we wanted the mayor to see how his decision would affect him. In our appeal we practiced Esther's four principles: We had the right appearance, the right spirit, the right timing and the right approach.

Would you like to know what happened? A few weeks later my secretary told me that a man in the church lobby wanted to see me and that the receptionist had said that he looked like Mayor Mike Dow. Mayor Dow came into my office, sat down on the couch and said, "Aaron, I have not slept very well since you asked me how gambling would affect my family, and I want you to be the first to know that I have decided to change my mind. You're right; gambling will affect our families adversely."

The next morning the mayor's decision was front-page news and a political firestorm erupted against him, but he survived and has become one of the most popular mayors in the "new South." In fact, the Civitan Club recently awarded Mayor Dow the title "Mobilian of the Year."

Encounter at the Convenience Store

Let me share one more story about the power of the appeal. When I first came to Mobile in the early '90s, I began stopping at the convenience store near our church every morning at 6:15 for a "wake me up" cup of coffee before going to our early morning prayer meeting.

Van, the store manager, has a fun personality and we traded barbs every morning about why he never came to my church, or how hard it was getting up that day, or why the Chicago Cubs can't seem to make it into the World Series. You know, the usual chitchat of the early morning risers. After a year of getting to know Van, a gentleman came to my office with a petition he asked me to sign. Local residents were concerned that Van's store carried pornographic magazines, and many young school children stopped by the store after school to buy snacks. The group was preparing to picket Van's store.

I told the man that the concern was valid and asked him a simple question: "Have you made a godly appeal to Van yet?" He said that he had not. I told him I could not, in good conscience, sign the petition until I chatted with my friend Van.

A few minutes later I drove over to the store and talked with Van about the situation. I was not arrogant or super-spiritual. I just appealed to him about the possibility of removing the magazines from the store. Van said, "I hate this trash as much as anyone, but it's storewide policy so I will have to take your appeal to my district manager."

Like to know what happened? Within one hour the magazines were off the shelves of that convenience store. As an act of good will, I appealed to our congregation to purchase their gasoline from Van to show our support for him and his bold decision even when he feared his business might suffer due to the drop in revenue.

A few months later he informed me that, to his surprise, because of the increased gasoline sales his business had increased.

That was ten years ago. Since then, I led Van to Christ. Recently, when I went in to pay for my gasoline, Van told me that the national office had just decided to pull the pornographic magazines off the shelves of all of their four thousand stores across the country. Van felt as if his decision was a seed sown to change a national policy. What a powerful, humble appeal will do!

In my lifetime I have made many appeals and others have come to me with their appeals. I try never to forget what it is like being in the position of asking for mercy and favor. So I have always sought as a leader to maintain a "yes" attitude. Oh, sometimes I am taken advantage of but not often.

Can I be honest? I think the reason people do not ask for favor more often is that they have a "no" attitude. They know that they would never show favor to someone asking for the same thing. I have heard some people say with pride, "I've never asked for anything." To me, this is neither noble nor inspiring. It is my guess that these same people have probably never given much either. But people with the spirit of "yes" know how blessed it is to show favor when someone appeals to them. No, not every appeal should be granted, but follow the leading of the Holy Spirit and respond accordingly.

Remember, there is someone in your life at this very moment that God has called to show you favor, promote you and even perhaps right a wrong for you. He or she is awaiting your appeal.

First, however, you need to make your requests and appeals in the heavenly throne room. Ask God for a strategy, and when His peace overtakes you, move out boldly in His perfect timing and make your appeal. Be sure that no anxiety, frustration or sense of entitlement is lingering somewhere in a corner of your heart.

And, like Esther, be prepared with the right appearance, the right spirit, the right timing and the right approach.

8

How to Cancel Judgments against You

Have you experienced moments in your journey when nothing seems to be going right? Is an unseen chain pulling you in reverse? Have your dreams and goals sputtered to a slow crawl?

Dear one, you may be living under a curse. Forget the schoolyard rhyme "Sticks and stones may break my bones but words will never hurt me." Words are powerful. Words of peace can end violence; words that curse can destroy.

Words do not have to be printed in large type on a billboard to have impact. Sometimes people speak things about us in secret and we feel the effect. We might not know the source or even the words, but we feel defenseless and confused. We know we are hurting but we are not sure why. Our passion for Jesus is high and we are following in Esther's footsteps, becoming His beautiful Bride, but turmoil seems to be blocking our paths to favor.

More likely than not judgments, or curses, are affecting us. The astonishing thing is that judgments spoken against us by others are just one side of the coin. On the other side are the inner vows and judgments we have spoken against ourselves. We may soon forget that we have denounced our own abilities or derided our walk with Christ—or spoken any one of a hundred other judgments against ourselves—but those words are out there, still fully armed and dangerous.

You might say that these curses spoken against us are like landmines buried in a forgotten war and lying dormant until an unsuspecting traveler happens by. One step brings an end to the journey.

Esther has walked the first minefield safely. When we saw her last, she took her life in her hands, approached the king and revealed the identity of her great enemy, Haman. And the result? The king, full of wrath at Haman's presumption, has him hanged on the gallows that Haman had prepared for Mordecai. Justice is served! Esther has won a great victory, but she is not out of danger. She might still lose the war.

But how could this be? Esther walks a godly path: She has been anointed with myrrh, walks in two-dimensional obedience, trusts in God's deliverance and enlargement program, stands in a spirit of agreement and has just made a successful godly appeal to the king for the protection of her people. Everything seems to be going well for Esther now, right? A quick glance at the opening of chapter 8 might indicate that a celebration is in order:

> On that day King Ahasuerus gave Queen Esther the house of Haman, the enemy of the Jews. And Mordecai came before the king, for Esther had told how he was related

to her. So the king took off his signet ring, which he had taken from Haman, and gave it to Mordecai; and Esther appointed Mordecai over the house of Haman.

Esther 8:1–2

Wow! Esther receives the entire estate of—with the exception of the king—probably the richest man in the Persian empire. Talk about a day to rejoice! And Mordecai receives the king's signet ring, a symbol of the king's authority. Mordecai also gets to live in Haman's house and manage all of Haman's wealth. Indeed, things are looking up for the Jews.

Words in the Way

Ah, but wise Esther sees beyond the euphoria of the moment. The good news is that Haman has been disarmed and hanged on the gallows, but the bad news is that the decree he wrote was sealed with the king's signet ring and mailed from the royal post office to the 127 districts of the empire. The decree is still legally binding and protected from alteration under the law of the Medes and Persians.

A decree—words on a paper—stands in her way. What she does next moves her beyond partial victory into complete victory. In other words, don't break out the party favors just yet to celebrate the Jews' good fortune. Just below the surface of this major breakthrough there is a bomb set to go off on the thirteenth day of the month of Adar. Haman is dead, but the enemies of the Jews are still sharpening their swords.

Not only that, but they are now more intent on their mission. Their beloved Haman is dead, their wicked scheme has been exposed and they are angry. If this decree is not overcome and its explosive power canceled, then only destruction awaits Esther and her people, estate and signet ring or not.

You might say that though Esther seems to be free, she is legally bound to an enemy's decree against her.

Esther knows that the curse must be broken and she approaches the king again with her next appeal:

> Now Esther spoke again to the king, fell down at his feet, and implored him with tears to counteract the evil plot of Haman the Agagite, and the scheme which he had devised against the Jews. And the king held out the golden scepter toward Esther. So Esther arose and stood before the king, and said, "If it pleases the king, and if I have found favor in his sight and the thing seems right to the king and I am pleasing in his eyes, let it be written to revoke the letters devised by Haman, the son of Hammedatha the Agagite, which he wrote to annihilate the Jews who are in all the king's provinces. For how can I endure to see the evil that will come to my people? Or how can I endure to see the destruction of my kindred?"
>
> Esther 8:3–6

Judgment is pending. Haman is dead, but a decree is a decree until it is canceled.

The Law Nailed to a Tree

Do you see the beautiful typology here? Jesus was hung on the tree instead of us. All of the punishment due to us was placed on Him. Galatians 3:13 says, "Cursed is everyone who hangs on a tree."

116

You see, the whole of the law was set against us. Colossians 2:13–14 says,

> And you, being dead in your trespasses and the uncircumcision of your flesh, He has made alive together with Him, having forgiven you all trespasses, having wiped out the handwriting of requirements that was against us, which was contrary to us. And He has taken it out of the way, having nailed it to the cross.
>
> Colossians 2:13–14

What an awesome truth! Christ Himself took the handwritten decree that was against us and nailed it to the cross. No trace of the decree is left because Christ has "wiped it out" or "blotted it out" as the King James Version renders it. It is completely erased.

Think of all of the many curses against us that were included in the decree that Christ nailed to His cross: sickness, bondage of all kinds, infirmity, fear, torment, dread, hopelessness and loneliness, just to mention a few.

Yet, even though this triumph and freedom were won for us on that cross, many still deal with unseen chains from the past and present that we cannot seem to break.

What is at issue here is that the cross of Jesus cancels out all decrees against us. But we have some work to do. Jesus wants us to be involved in the process. Notice the parallel with Esther. Jesus "disarmed principalities and powers, [and] . . . made a public spectacle of them, triumphing over them in it" (Colossians 2:15). At the same time He canceled out the handwritten decree that was against us.

Esther triumphed over Haman and made a public spectacle of him. Then on the same day she appealed to the king to revoke the written decree against her and the Jews.

Esther did not take her triumph over Haman for granted; she also took the necessary steps to cancel his written plans. This young woman had guts. Every time I read the account of her, I pray that you and I will enter the spiritual arena, wearing the king's ring and walking in the king's authority, and cancel out every decree that opposes us.

Think of it like this. When the children of Israel crossed the Jordan into the land that God had given them, they were commanded to possess the land through conquest and warfare. The same is true for us. Christ's cross provides for us the complete work of salvation, but we are called to appropriate its power in everyday living.

Your Involvement Needed

You might be asking, "Am I not protected from the enemy's destructive decrees?" Yes, of course you are if you are an overcoming believer walking in the fear of the Lord. Even so, there are two types of curses that can affect you. They require your involvement to cancel and annul them. These are decrees spoken against you by another believer, and inner vows and judgments that you have spoken against yourself.

Why is this? If you name the name of Christ and are living for Him then you are under the covenant of His blood. To bring a decree against us, Satan would have to pass through the blood of Jesus and this is impossible for Satan to do. So what is his scheme? How does he get around the blood? In the same way that Mordecai, Esther and Haman were all serving the same king in the same kingdom, Satan inspires a person already in the Kingdom, under the blood, who is wearing the signet ring of the Father's authority, to bring accusations against you. Or he provokes you to speak words against yourself.

First let's look at the curses that come from other believers and then we will look at the areas of judgments and inner vows.

Curses from Other Believers

I was born and raised near the San Francisco Bay area. Known for its breathtaking scenery and landmarks, San Francisco is also known for its witchcraft. A friend once relayed to me this story from an encounter with a witch.

My friend was a new convert to Christ and was attending a church in the Bay area that was filled with love and walking in unity. Soon after he began to attend, he noticed several changes in the attitude of the congregation. Accusations and rumors started surfacing about a host of different issues. People started leaving, and the church went into a tailspin. Months went by and there was no end to the bickering and squabbling. The pastor was perplexed about how this could happen to the church body he had taught so faithfully to forgive. He prayed and asked the Lord to reveal to him what was behind it.

Soon after, a woman who had been attending the church since the exact time the controversy began came to the pastor and confessed that she was a witch from a local witch coven. The leadership of her coven had realized that, try as they might, they could not bring curses on Christians because they could not get past the blood of Jesus! They had written hexes and spoken them to no avail. So they sent "missionaries" of conflict, rumor and hate to several churches in the area to spread accusations. The believers, unknowing, unaware, took the bait.

James says that with the tongue "we bless our God and Father, and with it we curse men, who have been made in the similitude [image] of God" (James 3:9). James is talking about believers here—Christian people who bless God and curse the people that He created in His image. And who is behind this destruction? Peter says, "Your adversary the devil walks about like a roaring lion, seeking whom he may devour" (1 Peter 5:8).

"Ah," you say, "he can never even so much as snip at me because I'm covered by the blood of Jesus."

Really? Notice what Paul the apostle says: "If you bite and devour one another, beware lest you be consumed by one another!" (Galatians 5:15).

Are you seeing the connection here? Satan is looking for someone to "devour," and, hungry as a lion, he tries but he cannot get past the blood of Jesus. So he inspires a believer to begin to curse and "bite" another believer, thus devouring him and eventually consuming him. Listen, we give the devil way too much credit. He cannot curse us; we, the Body of Christ, curse ourselves! He cannot devour us; we, the Body of Christ, devour ourselves!

Here is what the devil hopes will happen when we hear that someone has spoken an unkind word about us: We return evil for evil, insult for insult and cursing for cursing. We immediately defend ourselves by assaulting the character of the person bringing the accusation against us. Thus the vicious cycle begins of attack and counterattack. Duped by the scheme of Satan, we and our fellow believers engage in the conflict, and we wind up wounded in the minefield.

But suppose you have not fallen into that trap and yet it seems that the accusations and insults coming toward you are growing more pronounced, even more vicious.

People you have never offended are accusing you of things you have never thought about doing. Why? It is spirit against spirit. It is not you who offends them, it is the spirit of Jesus within you. You see, you are becoming more beautiful and irresistible to God. His favor and full authority of His Kingdom are being poured out upon you and the devil is devising evil schemes to roadblock your progress. If he can get you into an explosive minefield of controversy with other believers, then ultimately he will devour and consume you through their "biting" decrees and curses.

Today pastors are leaving church ministry at an alarming rate. More often than not, it is because of controversy. These men and women of God simply cannot handle the constant flow of rumor and accusations spoken against them and their families. "Well," some will say, "if you can't stand the heat then get out of the kitchen." But was the church ever meant to be a place of heated debate and controversy? Or was it ordained to be a place of love, acceptance and forgiveness? Curses and accusations inspired by the hurricane-strength demonic spirit of Satan can devour pastors and saints in the flocks.

If you are one of those trying to find your way in this inferno, please listen carefully. Like Esther you have a right and a responsibility to disarm the explosive power of curses and judgments spoken against you. If you do not, you may very well be devoured and consumed. I know this from firsthand experience.

Judgments Spoken Against You

Several years ago our church went through a difficult season. In most cases change is healthy even though it sometimes leaves a trail of tears for those not wanting an era to end. But progress cannot take place without the pain that change requires. Thus it was in our congregation. God was requiring us to make some changes in order to progress. Most people graciously and willingly embraced the changes, and some graciously and lovingly decided to worship elsewhere.

But a few people who left the church began a weekly telephone prayer meeting to ask the Lord to destroy my family and me. To this day I do not know who these people were because they never signed their letters of "encouragement." They only told me of their latest insight "from the Lord" concerning my downfall.

I know now that I should have been keenly aware of the damage those words would cause, but I was younger then and I did not understand the impact their curses would have upon me. I have since learned the power of a believer's tongue used for cursing rather than blessing. Jesus said in Acts 1:8, "You shall receive power when the Holy Spirit has come upon you." The Greek word that Jesus used here for *power* is the word *dunamis* whereby we get the word *dynamite*. James 3:6 says that the uncontrolled tongue of a believer "is a fire, a world of iniquity . . . and it is set on fire by hell." What do you get when you mix dynamite with a fiery tongue? Destruction!

After six months I was devoured and consumed by the decrees of destruction. My vision for the church began to suffer. I lost my passion for ministry and for teaching the Word of God. A deep, dark and demonic cloud began to hang over my home and my family and over our entire church. My wife and I did everything we could to break the heavy spirit. We prayed, we anointed our house with oil—inside and out. Want to know what happened? Absolutely nothing. My axe head had fallen off and was at the bottom of the Jordan River. I had lost my calling's edge.

After one year of this dark cloud hanging over me, a dear friend, Pastor Fred Roberts from Durbin, South Africa, came to preach at our church. After the morning service, we were walking up the sidewalk to my home to eat Chinese takeout food when Pastor Fred abruptly stopped and said something that changed my life.

"Aaron, you have too many people cursing you, so you must condemn their tongues." My mouth literally fell open because I had absolutely no idea what Pastor Fred was talking about.

"What do you mean, condemn their tongues?" I asked. He immediately quoted Isaiah 54:17: "'No weapon formed against you shall prosper, and every tongue which rises against you in judgment you shall condemn. This is the heritage of the servants of the LORD, and their righteousness is from Me,' says the LORD."

Right then and there I realized that in all of the time I had lived under the dark cloud of oppression, I had not taken the responsibility—my rightful "heritage" as a servant of the Lord—to cancel the decrees spoken against me by condemning the tongues of judgment and destruction. Pastor Fred agreed with me in prayer right there on the spot and I canceled the curses in Jesus' name. The Chinese food was cold that Sunday afternoon, but on that day the cloud lifted from my family and our congregation and everything began to turn around.

Now, whenever I sense in the spirit that a curse is coming my way, I immediately condemn the tongue of judgment and cancel the decree.

The Inner Vow

Another type of curse that we are responsible to contend with is the kind we bring upon ourselves. This happens through inner vows based on judgments we make toward others. Once we make these vows we usually soon forget them, but they too are legally binding landmines that need to be diffused.

Normally a vow is spoken against an authority figure in our lives, such as a parent, teacher or another caregiver. The judgment and resulting vow are usually declared when we are abused or mistreated by that individual.

A person with an abusive, alcoholic father, for instance, might say something like, "I will never be like my father." Yet, surprisingly, the son (or daughter) who spoke those words becomes an alcoholic as well as an abusive parent. What happened? Because he took a vow, he unleashed upon himself the exact same sin of the one being judged. This kind of curse fulfills the words of Jesus in Matthew 7:1–2: "Judge not, that you be not judged. For with what judgment you judge, you will be judged; and with the same measure you use, it will be measured back to you."

I have known people who are consistently in the hole financially. When I counsel them concerning their finances, oftentimes we can trace the core issues of their financial problems back to a vow and judgment that they spoke against their parents: "I'll never be poor like my parents." Our words can have lasting effects on us.

Dear one, please take a few moments and cancel out any tongue (yours included!) that has risen against you in judgment. Know that I and others have already prayed for the readers of this book as you face your moment. I believe that you will be as bold as Queen Esther as you free yourself from all of the vows and judgments against you.

In the next chapter, continuing to follow Esther's lead, we will learn how to write decrees that influence our future. It is vitally important, therefore, to cancel out any judgments spoken against our destinies before we move on. The following is an example of a prayer of deliverance:

> Father, I come to You in the mighty name of Jesus Christ, Your only Son. I ask You to forgive me for all of the words that I have spoken against myself and others and I release those whom I have cursed (myself included) from the condemning judgments that have come from my tongue.

It is very important at this point to allow the Holy Spirit to bring to your remembrance the curses that you have spoken and the destructive vows you have made. As the Holy Spirit reminds you, deal with each one individually, first repenting and then releasing yourself or another person from the curse.

When you have completed this stage of the prayer then pray the words of Isaiah 54:17:

> "No weapon formed against you shall prosper, and every tongue which rises against you in judgment you shall condemn. This is the heritage of the servants of the LORD, and their righteousness is from Me," says the LORD.

Then continue:

> Now, Lord, being freed and forgiven from all judgments, curses and vows I have spoken against myself and others, and freeing those held in the vice grip of my words,

I now forgive and bless those who have spoken against my destiny and purpose. And I accept my responsibility to condemn any tongue of judgment that speaks against Your divine will being accomplished in my future. In Jesus' name. Amen!

9

GATEWAYS INTO OUR FUTURE

Then King Ahasuerus said to Queen Esther and Mordecai the Jew, . . . "You yourselves write a decree for the
Jews, as you please, in the king's name, and seal it with
the king's signet ring; for a letter which is written in the
king's name and sealed with the king's signet ring no one
can revoke."

Esther 8:7–8

Washington, D.C., is beautiful in the springtime. The cherry trees that line the banks of the Tidal Basin at the foot of the Jefferson Memorial are in full bloom, and their fragrance adds a splendid note to an early April stroll. On a recent trip to the city named for our first president, I took in the sights and monuments that portray the greatness of our country.

Each of the memorials, museums and landmarks is breathtaking, not only for its architecture or because of what is inside, but because of what it represents: our democracy and our freedoms, bought with a great price.

One of the highlights is the National Archives building. It is in the rotunda of this building that you can gaze upon our most revered documents. I am speaking, of course, about the Declaration of Independence and the Constitution of the United States of America. The charters of our freedom are preserved in an encasement of pure titanium that can withstand fire, vandalism, even nuclear war. The documents are surrounded by argon, an inert gas that slows the aging process, so that guests can view them for years to come.

Our Constitution, signed by 39 people including Alexander Hamilton, Benjamin Franklin and George Washington, stands as a legal testament of the laws of the American Republic. It is interesting to watch the faces of those in line as they take their turn to gaze into the vault. The middle school and high school students from across the country, having learned the significance of this decree, approach with almost holy awe and reverence. The senior citizens approach the document with the same knowledge but with perhaps a deeper sense of appreciation, having enjoyed for a longer span of time the freedoms that the Constitution proclaims.

As I waited my turn I wondered why there was such a quiet respect in the rotunda. It was as if I were visiting a shrine rather than a glass case holding a piece of antique parchment paper. But then it dawned on me. We were not waiting in line as an act of patriotism or even historic inquiry, for that matter. We were there to honor the names and lives of our forefathers who had the good sense to put in writing their God-inspired ideas about freedom and democracy.

By far, apart from the Bible, the Declaration of Independence and the Constitution of the United States are the most revered writings in America. Other nations that were conceived with good intentions have fallen because either they never put their thoughts or laws into writing or they never preserved them by establishing a judicial branch of government to protect and defend them. I am grateful that our forefathers documented, signed and defended their concept of a free Republic in the birthing of our young nation.

Writing It Down

We saw from our last chapter the importance of revoking and canceling verbal assaults and written decrees against us. In order to do that, however, a new decree must be in writing as well. That is why Esther asked King Ahasuerus, "Let it be written to revoke the letters devised by Haman" (Esther 8:5).

A proclamation usually declares something verbally, but if it is not put into writing it holds little weight in a court of law. Webster's dictionary defines a *proclamation* this way: "An official formal public announcement." Webster's defines a *decree* this way: "An order having the force of law; to determine or order judicially." A decree, as it is used in Esther and elsewhere in the Bible, is simply a proclamation in written form.

Without a record of the proclamation in written form, there would be no proof of having created the law or declaration. That is why the Constitution and the Declaration of Independence remain such hallowed documents. Our

129

forefathers had the foresight to preserve freedom for future generations by writing down their concepts of democracy, signing the documents and then establishing a judicial branch and armed forces to defend them.

If you want an international passport, try going to the courthouse and proclaiming to the official who oversees the passport department, "I'm alive, you see. My heart is beating to prove it. And my parents have proclaimed to me for years that I was born in this country." The official will never issue a U.S. passport based on the verbal proclamation of your parents that you were indeed born on American soil. It will not matter, either, that your heart is beating, proving that you at one time were given life.

Thank goodness your parents signed your birth certificate and that it was recorded legally at the courthouse in the city or county of your birth. You see, proclamation or not, heartbeat or not, if you do not have it in writing, you cannot even prove you were born.

When we purchase a car the title is recorded with the state. When we purchase a home or property the deed is recorded. When we are joined in marriage we receive a marriage decree or license from the state. When we graduate from college we receive a diploma. The diploma is a written decree that proclaims the expertise conferred upon us by the educational institution that we attended.

It seems that we only gain access into our future success by the power of a written decree. A written decree acts as a passport into our future. We can have heart and even great faith, but having in hand a legal document will certainly make our entrance into our future destiny much more efficient.

The Power of the Pen

I am so thankful that God put His Word to man into writing, aren't you? I am thankful that holy men of old "wrote" as they were carried along by the Holy Spirit. I am glad Paul the apostle said, "See with what large letters I am writing" rather than, "Hear with what loud words I am speaking."

I am also very delighted that God took the time to write my name in the Lamb's Book of Life. He also records every one of our tears (see Psalm 56:8) and the times we meditate upon His name (see Malachi 3:16).

Esther knew that she would succeed through the power of the pen. That is why she pleaded with the king to write a new decree. As we read in the verse earlier, the king gave the queen and Mordecai permission to write a decree of their own.

The next verses tell us that the king's scribes were called and Mordecai dictated a decree, copies of which were sent to the leaders and citizens of the 127 provinces from India to Ethiopia,

> to every province in its own script, to every people in their own language, and to the Jews in their own script and language. And he wrote in the name of King Ahasuerus, sealed it with the king's signet ring, and sent letters by couriers on horseback, riding on royal horses bred from swift steeds. By these letters the king permitted the Jews who were in every city to gather together and protect their lives—to destroy, kill, and annihilate all the forces of any people or province that would assault them, both little children and women, and to plunder their possessions.
>
> Esther 8:9–11

Esther was a queen in a land that recognized governmental authority. She understood that putting her faith decree into writing was of utmost importance. We need to learn the lesson Esther teaches us.

Kingly Authority

You might ask, "How will my written decree ever become law? I'm not in a place of high authority like Esther." Indeed you are! You have come into the Kingdom of Jesus Christ for such a time as this. There is a grand purpose for you. There is a grand purpose for your family. You have been given the keys to the entire Kingdom. Your advancement in authority and influence can come through the pen. Revelation 1:6 says, "[Jesus] has made us kings and priests to His God and Father, to Him be glory and dominion forever and ever. Amen."

Each of us has a dual role. We are to rule with Christ under His Kingdom dominion as kings in the marketplace of this world. We are called, as well, to serve in His vineyard, ministering as priests to those in our sphere of influence.

So we have a kingly role and a priestly role. It is in my kingly role that I write my decrees. That is what kings do. They record the initiatives of their administration and establish them as law. They also chronicle their exploits and their achievements. Ecclesiastes 8:4 says, "Where the word of a king is, there is power." Proverbs 8:15 says, "By [wisdom] kings reign, and rulers decree justice." A person with a kingly calling, then, reigns by decreeing justice. You might even say, "A king reigns by writing it down."

If you look up the words *write*, *written* or *writing* in the Scriptures, you will find more references in Esther than in any other book of the Bible. Esther reigned by writing decrees that changed the future of the Jewish people.

A New Doctrine? No!

Now I know what you are thinking: "Is Aaron attempting to establish a new doctrine here? Is he saying that I must transcribe my faith proclamations into writing in order for God to work deliverance and enlargement on my behalf?" By all means, no. Writing a decree is not a prerequisite for breakthrough. Putting a faith proclamation into the written form of a decree—under the direction of the Holy Spirit—is simply working something out in the physical that you are declaring in the spiritual.

Let's take a moment to underline a basic principle: God recognizes our physical actions. You might think that writing a few sentences will not make a difference, but you will see in this chapter and the next that throughout the Scriptures those who put their decrees in writing got God's attention. Make no mistake: Decrees are powerful.

Take 2 Kings 13:13–19. Elisha instructed Joash, the king of Israel, to open an east window and shoot out an arrow as a sign of the Lord's deliverance over the Syrians. That done, Elisha then instructed Joash to take the remaining arrows and strike the ground with them. Joash struck the ground three times and stopped. I believe he probably felt foolish striking the floor with a handful of arrows. But there was a method to Elisha's madness. He was trying to help Joash declare in the natural what God was prepared to do in the supernatural.

Elisha was angry at the king's reluctance to move in expressive faith and he said, "You should have struck five or six times; then you would have struck Syria till you had destroyed it! But now you will strike Syria only three times" (2 Kings 13:19).

Elisha made a direct connection between our physical acts of faith and their ultimate fulfillment.

Now does this mean that we need to keep a quiver of arrows handy? No, but it does mean we should be open to the fact that physical acts of faith get God's attention.

How about the four friends of the paralytic in Mark 2 who tore the roof off a crowded house and lowered their buddy down into the room where Jesus was teaching? The Scripture records that "Jesus saw their faith." Their faith joined with the faith of the paralytic himself, who obeyed Jesus and received his healing by picking up his bed. That physical act of breaking through a roof was faith in action, and Jesus always recognizes faith when He sees it.

Likewise it was by faith that Zacchaeus climbed a sycamore tree and got Christ's attention; it was by faith that the woman with the issue of blood pressed through the crowd and touched the fringes of His garment and was healed instantly.

Take Your Faith Higher

If we accept this principle, that actions can express our faith, then putting our proclamations into the written form of a decree takes our faith to a new level. In writing a decree we are saying, "I trust so completely that God is going to work in my behalf that I am putting it in writing as proof of my faith!"

Job's "comforters" may have gotten a lot wrong, but one of them hit the nail on the head with this observation: "Thou shalt make thy prayer unto him, and he shall hear thee. . . . Thou shalt also decree a thing, and it shall be established unto thee" (Job 22:27–28, KJV).

Do you see? A faith proclamation that is written down leaves no doubt concerning exactly what you believe God will do. It gives you something in hand that you can refer to when future doubt may challenge your faith. It is a legal document written in the authority of Jesus' name that is proof of your deliverance. Also, when the miracle you are decreeing is fulfilled, you have a written testament of the faithfulness of God. And, equally important, putting your faith proclamations into writing is scriptural.

The leaders of the early Church knew the value of writing decrees. To secure a solid future for the infant Church, the apostles and elders in Jerusalem sent out written decrees concerning the principles of doctrine, church life and worship. The written decrees helped each church body to be set in scriptural order, and as a result they were enlarged and prospered:

> And as they went through the cities, they delivered to them the decrees to keep, which were determined by the apostles and elders at Jerusalem. So the churches were strengthened in the faith, and increased in number daily.
>
> Acts 16:4–5

Throughout the Word of God we are instructed and encouraged to write anointed and well-thought-out faith decrees. Here is a classic example. Habakkuk the prophet is watching and praying and listening to the Holy Spirit's direction for the future of Israel. He says, "I will stand my watch and set myself on the rampart, and watch to see what He will say to me" (Habakkuk 2:1).

Before the Lord delivers His Word to this man of God, however, He gives him a direct command, "Then the LORD answered me and said: 'Write the vision and make it plain on tablets, that he may run who reads it'" (Habakkuk 2:2). God tells Habakkuk to write down the decree so that messengers can carry it to others who will also benefit from its message.

And the list goes on. God tells the children of Israel that their passport to enlargement in their future will come in part because of writing: "And you shall write them [His decreed commands] on the doorposts of your house and on your gates, that your days and the days of your children may be multiplied in the land" (Deuteronomy 11:20–21).

Old Testament prophecies indicate that the Messiah will be born in Bethlehem of Judea. Mary and Joseph, however, live in Nazareth even into her ninth month of pregnancy. What is Mary doing in Nazareth? And what on earth would inspire a pregnant woman to ride a donkey all the way down to Bethlehem from Nazareth?

Remember, decrees can help initiate fulfilled promises, and it was a written decree that brought Mary and Joseph southward. Listen to the familiar words:

> And it came to pass in those days that a decree went out from Caesar Augustus that all the world should be registered. This census first took place while Quirinius was governing Syria. So all went to be registered, everyone to his own city. And Joseph also went up from Galilee, out of the city of Nazareth, into Judea, to the city of David, which is called Bethlehem, because he was of the house and lineage of David, to be registered with Mary, his betrothed wife, who was with child.
>
> Luke 2:1–5

Once again God uses the written decree of a king to fulfill a promise.

In fact, God loves to write. Remember the story of the handwriting on the wall in the book of Daniel? The fingers of a hand sent from God appear in wicked King Belshazzar's palace and write a decree on the wall. This action initiates the fall of his empire and the deliverance of the Jews from Babylonian captivity.

It is also the finger of God that writes in the sand in front of an angry mob about to stone a woman caught in adultery. I am not sure what Christ wrote in the earth that day, but the power of His written decree initiated deliverance for the woman.

And don't forget the Ten Commandments! Knowing that the children of Israel would forget the verbal proclamation of His commandments, God writes them down in the form of a decree. Also Moses takes the time to write down "all the words of the LORD" (Exodus 24:4).

Jesus commanded John the revelator, "What you see, write . . ." (Revelation 1:11). And in the future Christ Himself will write upon us the name of God, the name of the city of God and His new name (see Revelation 3:12).

If you stand at the Western Wall in Jerusalem today, you will see thousands of Jewish prayer warriors writing down their faith decrees and placing them in the cracks of the wall. They understand the power of a written faith decree.

We will study in the next chapter how to go about writing decrees, but let me share here a contemporary example of how a Holy Spirit-inspired written decree can take our faith higher.

My sister, Kathy, wanted desperately to buy her own home. She had two small children, no savings and a small income. No chance, you might say. She called realtors, but once she told them her story, they never called back. Without the money for a down payment, or even closing costs, a home purchase was just a dream. But Kathy was convinced that God wanted her to have a home.

One day she wrote on a piece of paper exactly what she wanted: how many bedrooms, bathrooms, square feet, the neighborhood she wanted, at a price she could afford . . . with no down payment. She put the note under her pillow, and she prayed.

Four days later she opened the Sunday paper and read a "for sale by owner" classified ad. Amazed she read it again. The classified was almost word for word what she had written in her decree. It even ended with these words, "No down payment? Don't worry." Two months later, Kathy and her family were living in that house.

If you are waiting on God for future direction and God begins to decree in your spirit concerning your tomorrows, by all means write it down. Your faith will soar.

"And It Was Found Written . . ."

Now let us return to the story of Esther and Mordecai and see how decrees changed their future.

We have reviewed the decree written by Haman that threatened to annihilate the Jews. Do you realize, though, that it was the record of an earlier event that began the flow of justice and favor toward the Jews? Had not this event been documented, the story of Esther would have had a much different ending. I am referring, of course, to the uncovering of the plot of Bigthan and Teresh to assassinate Ahasuerus, told in the second chapter of Esther. We learned that Mordecai heard of it and informed Queen

Esther, who told the king. The co-conspirators were hanged on the gallows.

Now remember what happened to the record of that event? "It was written in the book of the chronicles in the presence of the king" (Esther 2:23). What do kings do? They chronicle and decree! And it is a good thing that Ahasuerus and his scribes were good at keeping records, because it was the review of that event during the king's sleepless night that led to Mordecai being honored on the very morning that Haman had planned for him to be executed.

I love those words describing this event: "And it was found written . . ." (Esther 6:2). If the king had failed to write down Mordecai's good deed then the memory of it would have been lost. Had the king failed to fulfill his kingly duty to chronicle and decree the events of his rule, would Mordecai have been hanged on the gallows rather than honored in the city square? You decide. One thing is clear, however—the pen is a powerful instrument indeed.

We begin to see that decrees that are inspired by the Holy Spirit can act as gateways into our future and keep us from wandering or losing focus. A decree written in faith can set a boundary line the enemy cannot cross.

God set boundary lines at the time of creation with a perpetual decree that is still at work today:

"Do you not fear Me?" says the LORD. "Will you not tremble at My presence, who have placed the sand as the bound of the sea, by a perpetual decree, that it cannot pass beyond it? And though its waves toss to and fro, yet they cannot prevail; though they roar, yet they cannot pass over it."

Jeremiah 5:22

We, too, can write decrees that set the boundaries for the turbulent waves of life so that we can remain in safe harbor.

Your Charter of Freedom

Don't be fooled. Satan himself knows the powerful value of a written decree. He already has plans to write his decree of personal ownership, "the mark of his name" (Revelation 14:11), on the foreheads and palms of multitudes in the near future. Certainly he knows the ultimate power of the pen.

But God will preserve the righteous.

Ezekiel has an awesome vision of how God will do this:

> Then He called out in my hearing with a loud voice, saying, "Let those who have charge over the city draw near, each with a deadly weapon in his hand." And suddenly six men came from the direction of the upper gate, which faces north, each with his battle-ax in his hand. One man among them was clothed with linen and had a writer's inkhorn at his side. They went in and stood beside the bronze altar.
>
> Ezekiel 9:1–2

All of these men are mighty warriors indeed. One of them, however, is prepared not only for warfare but also for writing, because at his side hangs an inkhorn. Whenever I picture this mighty man of God in Ezekiel's vision, I always think of the famous quote by Edward Bulwer Lytton, "Beneath the rule of men entirely great, the pen is mightier than the sword."

To this man clothed in linen who has the writer's ink-horn at his side, the Lord had a special assignment:

> "Go through the midst of the city, through the midst of Jerusalem, and put a mark on the foreheads of the men who sigh and cry over all the abominations that are done within it."
>
> Ezekiel 9:4

God preserved the righteous by writing a decree of some kind upon their foreheads.

Is there an Esther in this generation who will dip her writing instrument into the inkhorn and decree protection for the people of God? Is there a mother or father reading these words who will, like Esther, understand that partial victory is not nearly good enough and take the time to write a decree that their children will serve the living God in the midst of a wicked and perverse culture?

Today many fear that our attention spans have collapsed and that the words of writer Tillie Olsen have come true: "We are in a time of more hidden and foreground silences, women and men. Denied full writing."

I would like to challenge these words because I believe that as you read this book you will, like Esther, come to understand that you have been called to the Kingdom for such a time as this and, like Queen Esther, begin to rule by writing faith decrees. You can fulfill the words of William Wordsworth and take up "the feather, whence the pen was shaped . . . dropped from an angel's wing."

Listen to the words of other famous writers who believed that the pen was mightier than the sword:

> "A pen is certainly an excellent instrument to fix a man's attention and to inflame his ambition," wrote John Adams.

141

"Reading maketh a full man, conference a ready man, and writing an exact man," wrote Francis Bacon.

"The Lord created heaven and earth and as an immediate afterthought, writers," reasoned Fred De Cordova.

"Self-expression must pass into communication for its fulfillment," wrote Pearl S. Buck.

"Devise, wit, write, pen," wrote William Shakespeare.

"Anybody can make history—only a great man can write it," proclaimed Oscar Wilde.

"I put a piece of paper under my pillow, and when I could not sleep I wrote in the dark," explained Henry David Thoreau.

"We have talked long enough in this country about equal rights. We have talked for a hundred years or more. It is time now to write the next chapter—and to write in the books of law," declared Lyndon Bains Johnson.

Are you convinced yet that there is power in the pen? You might be asking, "Why write down my verbal faith proclamations? God Himself simply spoke the Word of faith and by them framed the worlds." True indeed. But remember He also put His proclamation in writing; otherwise the record of Creation would have been lost.

The Constitution and the Declaration of Independence are not infallible like the Holy Bible, but we do know that as the framers of these documents wrote, they prayed and asked God for direction in writing the decrees that have preserved freedom on our shores for more than twenty decades now. We would agree with the framers who said, "God is involved in the affairs of men."

So why can't you write a personal constitution concerning God's specific purpose and calling upon your life? Why can't you write a family decree that describes the gifts and callings you see in each one of your children? Why can't you write a declaration of independence from the boundaries and bondages the adversary has placed upon you? Why can't you write a decree of justice when you have been falsely accused? Oh, your encasement may not be made of pure titanium, high-strength glass, specially treated aluminum and surrounded by argon gas, but it will be no less inspired by the hand of God than the charters of freedom in the National Archives.

You might encase your decrees in a file you can easily open from time to time to make sure you are still on course with the things God has declared to you about your future. You might put your decree under your pillow as my sister did. Your decrees might even be written in the back of your Bible. What better encasement than that!

Our next chapter is very practical, and in it I will show you how to write decrees. Grab your pen!

10

HOW TO WRITE DECREES

Congratulations! We have made it. In our journey
we have seen that the King desires to display the
beauty of His Bride—you and me—to the world.
But in order for us to walk in kingly rule and authority
during this final triumphant procession of the Church, we
must follow in Esther's footsteps. We must commit to the
process of becoming beautiful before we enter into the
procession. We must submit to the myrrh anointing that
takes away all of our wrinkles and blemishes. We must
walk in two-dimensional obedience to both God and man.
We must be willing to enter into spiritual conflict and refuse
to live in the false security of the palace.

Wait, the list goes on. We must trust in God's will not only
to deliver us from our Hamans but to enlarge our territory.
We must stand in a spirit of unity and cooperation with

those around us. We must appeal to those in authority by having the right appearance, the right spirit, the right timing and the right approach. We must have the faith that it takes to believe that God will protect us and turn our gallows into gain. We must develop a tenacity to reverse written and verbal judgments. And, finally, we must understand the power of the pen and the justice that can be released through our written decrees. We will soon see in our final chapter how Esther's decree established a day on the Jewish calendar that instructed all of Israel to celebrate their good fortune in the reversal of Haman's curse. Indeed, Esther changed history by her willing, obedient heart.

If it all seems like a pretty tall order, remember this. A Jewish slave girl took this climb before us. If she had missed one step along the way, she would not have saved her people, or herself.

Got a pen? Now comes the fun part. Are you ready to write a decree that will change your future?

Elements of a Decree

When I began to understand the power of the written decree, I started by simply writing down my thoughts during and after my prayer time. I wrote down the things God spoke to me concerning the future of everything under the influence of my kingly and priestly anointing. What does that include? My wife and children, the needs of our family, the needs of our church family, the needs of our community and things concerning my own personal gifts and callings.

As God began to unfold different aspects of my kingly and priestly role, I began to proclaim them in faith verbally during my prayer time. Afterward I simply put my faith proclamations into written form.

What are the basic rules of the road of a written decree? When you begin to write, ask the Lord to guide you. I think many people proclaim things they have never prayed about and then wonder why they never come to pass. Remember the verses from the book of Job that were quoted earlier: "Thou shalt make thy prayer unto him, and he shall hear thee. . . . Thou shalt also decree a thing, and it shall be established unto thee" (Job 22:27–28, KJV). This is the biblical progression: First pray and then decree.

Also remember that a decree is not authoritative like the Scriptures, but it can be a powerful tool in your hand if you have taken the time to receive the Holy Spirit's direction.

A decree is simply a point of reference for you. It moves your faith to a higher level when you take the time to put into writing the things God has already placed in your heart. When what you have decreed comes to pass by faith, then the written record acts as a concrete testimony to you concerning your journey of faith in a matter.

The decree never replaces your responsibility to walk in faith while the thing you decree is accomplished. Also remember that once you receive the guidance of the Holy Spirit to write a decree, God is going to work it out in His time. Do not try to force its fulfillment. It is the same as when you receive prophetic words: You do not need to try to cause their fulfillment. If it is a word from the Lord then the Lord will work it out. You simply do not need to worry about it.

There are many different kinds of decrees that you can write. We are going to look at ten of them:

protection decrees
remembrance decrees
decrees for your children

147

return to me/soulwinning decrees
justice decrees
covenant decrees
city decrees
stewardship/financial decrees
word decrees
life vision decrees

Protection Decrees

Did you know that you have probably written several protection decrees without realizing it? Every time you fill out insurance papers to protect your home, property and auto, you are signing a protection decree. Homeowner and automobile liability insurance protect you from lawsuits should someone slip on your driveway or be injured in a car accident that you might cause.

A biblical protection decree is very similar. This is what Mordecai did. His written protection decree was the basis for turning the curse of destruction away from the Jewish people: "And he wrote in the name of King Ahasuerus. . . . By these letters the king permitted the Jews who were in every city to gather together and protect their lives" (Esther 8:10–11).

A protection decree, therefore, is a declaration of God's covering over the people and things that concern you. When my wife and I send our teenage daughters on their summer missions projects, we not only pray protection over them but we decree it in writing. Mordecai decreed protection and the Jews lived to see another day.

We also decree protection over the people of our congregation. We decree that their children, possessions, businesses, spiritual gifts, finances, joy and commitment to Christ are all off-limits to the designs of Satan.

Remembrance Decrees

Esther wrote a decree of remembrance. She decreed that the memory of God's deliverance would be memorialized every year in a celebration known as the Feast of Purim. Esther's decree states

> that these days should be remembered and kept throughout every generation, every family, every province, and every city, that these days of Purim should not fail to be observed among the Jews, and that the memory of them should not perish among their descendants.
>
> Esther 9:28

By the way, the Feast of Purim is still celebrated faithfully by Jewish people all around the world.

We will study the decree of Esther in full in our next chapter, but let's look briefly here at the value and importance of a decree of remembrance. A remembrance decree should chronicle the details of how God brought you through a challenging life situation. You might open the decree with the words, "I (or we) decree that I will always remember how God worked on my behalf concerning. . . ."

The Psalms are filled with the remembrance decrees of King David. Hezekiah wrote a remembrance decree concerning the occasion of his healing, which is found in Isaiah 38. In Numbers 33, Moses wrote down the starting points of the journeys of the children of Israel through the wilderness so they would remember what God brought them through. The twelve stones mentioned in Joshua 4 acted as a remembrance decree concerning the crossing of the Jordan River. The children of Israel whitewashed the stones with lime and wrote on them all the words of the law.

God Himself has a book of remembrance. You will find good examples in Psalm 56:8; 139:16; and Malachi 3:16.

Remembrance decrees are all around us. Look, for example, at the many points of remembrance we celebrate here in the United States: Columbus Day, Veterans' Day, Memorial Day, Labor Day, Independence Day, Martin Luther King Jr. Day, Pearl Harbor Day, "a day that will live in infamy." And now September 11, 2001, has been decreed "the day we will never forget." These days are all focal points in our year that bring us to solemn and sober remembrance. Oh, and I can't forget Thanksgiving, a day decreed to be filled with thankfulness to God for His bountiful blessings on our nation.

We remember our family histories in photograph scrapbooks. How about remembering God's points of faithfulness in a book of remembrance? At the end of each year you can recall and record the triumphant moments of God's breakthroughs on your behalf. Can you imagine the impact a book of remembrance will have on your faith and the faith of others as you read the record of God's miraculous intervention and blessings, say, ten years from now?

Decrees for Your Children

Your children belong to God and He made each of them with unique gifts and callings. Isaiah said, "Here am I and the children whom the LORD has given me! We are for signs and wonders in Israel from the LORD of hosts, who dwells in Mount Zion" (Isaiah 8:18). At times we might have little faith or even hope that our kids are called to greatness, but, regardless, I as a parent am called to believe what God has decreed concerning my children. They are for "signs and wonders" in their generation.

Listen to what God says about our children. They are "like arrows in the hand of a warrior" (Psalm 127:4). "They shall not be ashamed, but shall speak with their enemies in the gate" (Psalm 127:5). They are "like olive plants all around your table" (Psalm 128:3). "Our sons may be as plants grown up in their youth; . . . our daughters may be as pillars, sculptured in palace style" (Psalm 144:12). "All your children shall be taught by the LORD, and great shall be the peace of your children" (Isaiah 54:13).

May we never be like Zacharias, who would not believe the angel Gabriel when told that his wife, Elizabeth, would bear a son named John. Nor would he believe that his son would be great in the sight of the Lord, would be filled with the Holy Spirit, would prepare the way for Christ in the spirit and the power of Elijah, and would make ready a people prepared for the Lord. As a result of his unbelief, he was unable to speak until eight days after John was born.

On that eighth day, the day when the baby was circumcised, something strange happened. It was traditional to name a son after his father, and the family members wanted to name the boy Zacharias. But Gabriel had said that the boy would be named John. Elizabeth persisted and said, "No, we're going to name him John."

Notice what happens next:

> But they said to her, "There is no one among your relatives who is called by this name." So they made signs to his father—what he would have him called. And he asked for a writing tablet, and wrote, saying, "His name is John." And they all marveled. Immediately his mouth was opened

and his tongue loosed, and he spoke, praising God. Then fear came on all who dwelt around them; and all these sayings were discussed throughout all the hill country of Judea. And all those who heard them kept them in their hearts, saying, "What kind of child will this be?" And the hand of the Lord was with him.

Luke 1:61–66

Zacharias asked for a pen and a pad and decreed in writing his son's name—going against his own unbelief of what the boy would later become and against his family's tradition for naming children.

This story of the father writing down and decreeing what his son's name would be, along with the other unusual events, was told throughout the hill country of Judea. The people said, "What kind of child will this be?" We should have this same expectancy about our children's futures.

I have written out the names of each of my children and then decreed the gifts and callings I see in each of their lives. I do not decree what they will do in life but rather who they are in God and what they will become as persons. I base the decree on the spiritual gifts that are already obviously working in their lives. I also decree that they will marry godly mates (if they desire to be married someday), experience the joy of the Lord all the days of their lives and that they will never grow cold to the things of God. Truly I believe in God's Word that promises, "Thou shalt also decree a thing, and it shall be established unto thee" (Job 22:28, KJV). Here is a portion of the decrees over our four children.

"Rachel, you are my firstborn daughter. Your name means 'beautiful' and I am grateful that you have chosen to keep your inner spirit as pure and beautiful as your countenance.

May your creative gift of writing grow ever stronger as you help transform your generation through the power of the pen. You are blossoming as a leader and have become a shining example for Christ and His Kingdom."

"Elizabeth, your name means 'oath of the Lord' and already I see your incredible commitment to share Christ's love with lost kids. Your vivacious personality keeps me smiling and assures me I was right in nicknaming you 'Lizzie.' You are definitely a girl with an appointment with destiny. Your strong gift in evangelism will bear much fruit for Jesus."

"Hannah, your name means 'graciousness' and grace can be interpreted as a gift. At ten years old you already show evidence that you have been 'graced' with gifts from the Lord. Your uncanny ability to remember small details and then express them in orderly sequence leads me to believe that you have a strong gift of teaching."

"Nathan, your name means 'gift from God' and your mom, three sisters and I would all agree that you are a gift to our family. The prophet Nathan was a gift from God in the life of King David; he spoke truth to a king in sin. Your destiny is to be a faithful friend who stands for truth when it is compromised. You, Nathan, are truly a gift to your generation."

There is another biblical example of parents who decreed the names of their children that I would like to relate.

In Isaiah 8, Jerusalem was surrounded by the armies of Syria and Ephraim. With the city under siege, the Lord commanded the prophet Isaiah to

"Take a large scroll, and write on it with a man's pen concerning Maher-Shalal-Hash-Baz. And I will take for Myself faithful witnesses to record, Uriah the priest and Zechariah the son of Jeberechiah." Then I went to the prophetess, and she conceived and bore a son. Then the LORD said to me, "Call his name Maher-Shalal-Hash-Baz; for before the child shall have knowledge to cry 'My father' and 'My mother,' the riches of Damascus and the spoil of Samaria will be taken away before the king of Assyria."

Isaiah 8:1–4

God was saying, "Isaiah, in the face of this challenging situation I want you and your wife to have a son and call him Maher-Shalal-Hash-Baz." The boy's name would turn out to be the longest name recorded in the Bible. How would you like to have that name? Though long and difficult to pronounce, the name is very significant. It means "speed up the return of our spoil." Not only did God tell Isaiah to give him this name, but He also told him to write it down as a decree. Isaiah did so and brought two men along with him to witness the writing of the decree. God said that before the child could say "Daddy" or "Mommy" their enemies would lose it all.

He wanted Isaiah to have the testimony of His faithfulness in hand prior to the miracle so that all would know that the return of the spoil was His working. Again, one more confirmation that a written decree is a point of reference of God's faithfulness before and after its fulfillment comes.

Isaiah's first son was named "Shear-Jashub" and his name means "a remnant shall return." The two names together were wonderful reminders to God's people that He had secured their future. It is at the end of this same chapter, in fact, that the prophet Isaiah sealed the decree among his disciples and began the process of waiting in faith for its fulfillment. He said: "Bind up the testimony, seal the law among my disciples" (Isaiah 8:16).

Notice that Isaiah understood that a written decree is a law that is irrevocable. By binding and sealing the decree

Isaiah had set into motion the same law of faith that Jesus gave us in Matthew's gospel: "Whatever you bind on earth will be bound in heaven, and whatever you loose on earth will be loosed in heaven" (Matthew 16:19).

I have often followed this same format in the decree process. If it is a decree for our church I will have at least two other leaders sign it with me. We then bind and seal it and place it in an envelope or folder. But more important, we seal it in prayer: "Lord, we believe that You are directing us in this step of faith and so we have written down our proclamation and we know by faith that it is now bound and sealed in heaven. In Jesus' name. Amen."

Next we file the decree and then wait patiently for it to be fulfilled, never giving up the spirit of prayer concerning the matter. After Isaiah had bound and sealed the decree and set the law of faith into motion he said, "Here am I and the children whom the LORD has given me! We are for signs and wonders in Israel from the LORD of hosts, who dwells in Mount Zion" (Isaiah 8:18). His children—"a remnant shall return" and "speed up the return of our spoil"—were signs to their generation of God's faithfulness.

You can write decrees about your children before they are born as Isaiah did. Also, as your children grow and mature you can write decrees concerning given points in their life journeys. You may not feel inclined to name your children Maher-Shalal-Hash-Baz or Shear-Jashub, but you can decree that they will be signs of God's faithfulness and workers of God's miraculous wonders in their times.

Return to Me/Soulwinning Decrees

You can write a decree that proclaims the return of a backslidden child, loved one or friend. Second Chronicles

30 records the story of King Hezekiah who sent a decree, via runners who carried letters, to all Israel that she should return to the Lord in keeping the Passover.

Israel as a nation was largely in a backslidden condition and so the written decree was forthright and intense: "Children of Israel, return to the LORD God of Abraham, Isaac, and Israel; then He will return to the remnant of you who have escaped from the hand of the kings of Assyria" (2 Chronicles 30:6). As the runners delivered the letters, some mocked and laughed, but many humbled themselves and came to Jerusalem to celebrate the feast of Passover.

A "return to me/soulwinning" decree is a declaration of faith that your backslidden, unsaved friend or loved one will return to Christ or respond to His love for the first time. Christ wants everyone to be saved and to come to the knowledge of the truth, so you are well within sound boundaries to decree their salvation. We know from Scripture that those who are born again were chosen in Christ before the foundation of the world and predestined to be conformed to His image.

At the time of choosing me, did God decree in writing that I would put my trust in Him? There is an interesting verse in Revelation 17:8 that says, "And those who dwell on the earth [the unsaved] will marvel, whose names are not written in the Book of Life from the foundation of the world." This verse seems to indicate that at the time when God by His foreknowledge predestined one to believe, He also wrote that one's name in the Book of Life. This, of course, would not nullify our free will to choose Christ or reject Him. Was God decreeing my salvation in writing before the foundation of the world? It is food for thought, is it not? Paul proclaimed to the Philippian jailer that he and his entire household would be saved, and consequently the whole family came to Jesus.

I mentioned Dr. Fred Roberts in an earlier chapter. He and his wife, Nelly, are dear friends and pastors of Durbin Christian Center in Durbin, South Africa. Recently they finished the completion of a new sanctuary, The Jesus Dome, which is the largest domed building in the Southern Hemisphere, seating ten thousand people.

Before the carpet layers came, Pastor Fred instructed his congregation to write the names of their unsaved family members and friends on the bare concrete floor of the building. Want to know what happened? One by one multitudes of these people have been swept into the Kingdom of God! Coincidence? I dare not think so. Remember: "Thou shalt also decree a thing, and it shall be established unto thee" (Job 22:28, KJV).

If your son or daughter is away from God, you can decree that he or she will come back. You could write something like: "Lord, I thank You for my son, Lou. I thank You that You knew him before the foundation of the world and You have a divine purpose for his life. I decree according to Your Word in Proverbs 22:6: 'Train up a child in the way he should go, and when he is old he will not depart from it.' I decree that Lou will not depart from Your mighty Word and that he will fulfill Your call upon his life. Thank You, Jesus, that Lou will stop running from Your presence and that You will make him uncomfortable in the way that he is now living. I decree that the enemy releases Lou from all bondage and control, and I decree that the Son of God will set Lou totally free. I decree this in the mighty name of Jesus Christ of Nazareth."

Now date the document and have another person who will pray in agreement with you sign it with you. Keep it in a secure place, a filing cabinet or even in your Bible. Don't give up in prayer. When your son comes to Christ, show him the document and it will be a testimony of the power of believing, decreeing prayer.

Justice Decrees

Proverbs 8:15 says, "By me [wisdom] kings reign, and rulers decree justice." It is in our kingly roles to decree justice. When King David reigned over all Israel, for instance, he administered judgment and justice to his people. This was done through decrees that set just laws into motion and brought justice to those who were wrongly treated or falsely accused.

Isaiah lamented the fact that in his day "no one [called] for justice" (Isaiah 59:4). Jeremiah looked ahead prophetically to Christ's day and proclaimed, "'Behold, the days are coming,' says the LORD, 'that I will raise to David a Branch of righteousness; a King shall reign and prosper, and execute judgment and righteousness in the earth'" (Jeremiah 23:5).

We are living in the days of "The Branch of righteousness." Jesus is releasing justice and judgment in the earth but He needs willing vessels to administer it. The Church one day will judge and govern the nations, so now is a good time to get started. It is time for us to call for justice.

Oftentimes in the Scriptures God brings justice to His people through a written decree. When Nebuchadnezzar, the king of Babylon, had crushed Israel and was carrying away her people captive, God did a remarkable thing. He decreed that justice would come to His people. Jeremiah 51 is one of many prophetic decrees of justice. Even as the Jews were being led into bondage God said, "Behold,

I will plead your case and take vengeance for you" (Jeremiah 51:36).

Jeremiah did something interesting. He took a scroll and wrote a decree concerning the just judgment that was going to come upon Babylon for her treatment of the people of God. Then he told Seraiah, one of the leaders of Israel being led away as a slave,

> "When you arrive in Babylon and see it, and read all these words, then you shall say, 'O LORD, You have spoken against this place to cut it off, so that none shall remain in it, neither man nor beast, but it shall be desolate forever.' Now it shall be, when you have finished reading this book, that you shall tie a stone to it and throw it out into the Euphrates. Then you shall say, 'Thus Babylon shall sink and not rise from the catastrophe that I will bring upon her.'"
>
> Jeremiah 51:61–64

Speaking through the prophet Isaiah, God said that He would dry up the rivers of Babylon and make the crooked places straight (see Isaiah 44:27; 45:2). When Cyrus the Great laid siege to Babylon, his engineers rerouted the Euphrates River by straightening it and directing it away from the city. They captured Babylon by marching on the dry riverbed underneath the city wall—thus walking directly on top of the decree that Jeremiah had written seventy years before and that now lay on the bottom of the Euphrates with a rock tied around it.

Some believe that on the same night that Cyrus and his army marched under the city walls of Babylon and fulfilled the written decree of God in Jeremiah 51, King Belshazzar, who had succeeded his father Nebuchadnezzar to the throne of Babylon, held his drunken feast. He commanded his servants to bring the gold and silver vessels taken from the Jerusalem Temple so that he and his lords, his wives and his concubines could drink from them.

As they drank and worshiped their gods, suddenly God declared his justice through another written decree. A man's hand sent from God appeared and wrote Babylon's just punishment on the walls of Belshazzar's palace: "God has numbered your kingdom, and finished it. . . . You have been weighed in the balances, and found wanting. . . . Your kingdom has been divided, and given to the Medes and Persians" (Daniel 5:26–28).

Jesus began His ministry by reading from the written decree of Isaiah that proclaimed that He had come to bring justice to the poor, the brokenhearted, the captives, the blind and the oppressed. When the scribes and Pharisees brought the woman caught in adultery to Jesus and demanded her execution, Christ the just Judge twice stooped down and wrote something on the ground. No one is sure what He wrote, but one thing is certain: It was a decree of justice. Each accuser walked away without stoning the woman to death.

In the awesome picture of Christ's return in Revelation 19, it is said that Christ, faithful and true, is coming as a righteous judge. But to administer justice legally there must be documentation in writing. So written on His robe and on His thigh (by the finger of God Himself, I believe) is this name: "King of kings and Lord of lords," sealing forever His legal power and authority to establish His just rule on the earth.

In Revelation 5 we see a beautiful picture of a justice decree. Jesus, the Lamb of God, takes from the hand of God the Father the written title deed of the earth. Though it appears that Satan has had his way in wreaking havoc on planet earth and is in full ownership of this globe, he is not. God has had in hand all along a written decree and deed to the earth, and only His Son is worthy of opening the seven seals and releasing God's just judgment, retaking full possession of the earth.

Before God administered justice in the Scriptures, He often decreed the coming justice prior to its fulfillment. Even at the Crucifixion, when Jesus was taking our sin upon Himself, God the Father made sure that this act of bringing justice to the world was in writing. A legal decree was written by the highest authority in the city of Jerusalem in Hebrew, Greek and Latin and it read, "Jesus of Nazareth, the King of the Jews" (John 19:19).

The Jewish leaders were upset with the decree and wanted to change its authoritative, factual wording: "The chief priests of the Jews said to Pilate, 'Do not write, "The King of the Jews," but, "He said, 'I am the King of the Jews.'"' Pilate answered, 'What I have written, I have written'" (John 19:21–22).

Would Christ's death that paid the penalty for our sin have been legally binding without Pilate's decree? Of course. But the written decree was nailed there as a statement of Christ's innocence in the face of injustice.

In addition, the written decree and accusations that stood opposed to us were also nailed to the cross. Colossians 2:14 states that Jesus "wiped out the handwriting of requirements that was against us, which was contrary to us. And He has taken it out of the way, having nailed it to the cross." So this decree by Pilate fittingly shows the power of the name and title that would revoke all legal accusations against those who would call upon the name of Jesus Christ, the King of the Jews.

Dear friend, if you have been accused of a wrong that you have not committed you can decree your justice. Christ has called us to be kings and priests and part of our role is to administer justice. It is time for you to set things in order.

As noted earlier in this book, God's people are being preyed upon and falsely accused as never before. Lawsuits abound against Christians, churches and Christian ministries. If you have been accused of a wrong then call for justice and decree it prior to its fulfillment.

Since teaching this principle in our church I have had several business people come to me and share the bogus charges that have been brought against them. We follow the example of Hezekiah when he was falsely accused: "And Hezekiah received the letter from the hand of the messengers, and read it; and Hezekiah went up to the house of the LORD, and spread it before the LORD" (2 Kings 19:14).

We pray in agreement that God will be merciful to all involved. Next we write the general details of the accusation on a piece of paper. After this we decree in writing that the accusations will not stand, that justice and truth will reign in the courtroom, that the false accuser will drop all charges and that the secret motivations of his heart will come to the surface. We then sign the decree and seal it with prayer.

In this process I have witnessed some incredible miracles and literally seen charges, accusations and lawsuits dropped. By the way, if you are guilty as charged, a decree for mercy would be the proper document to write.

Covenant Decrees

A covenant decree is simply a written vow that you make with God. We are not obligated to make vows, only to keep them if we have (see Ecclesiastes 5:4–5). A financial faith promise to missions is a covenant decree. Also a vow concerning any aspect of your relationship with God that is placed in written form is a covenant decree.

Joshua made a covenant decree when he proclaimed, "As for me and my house, we will serve the LORD" (Joshua 24:15). Later he put it into writing. You might consider a personal or family covenant decree concerning your willingness to serve Christ and follow His Word. Be certain before you do, however, that you fully intend to carry it out. If you have made a rash vow, ask the Lord's forgiveness.

City Decrees

A city decree is a written proclamation of faith over your city.

Most cities have slogans. Chicago is the "City That Never Sleeps." New York is the "Big Apple." Los Angeles is the "City of Angels." The original name of our city, Mobile, Alabama, was the "Bay of the Holy Spirit"! These slogans are interesting but often are not the original words written about a city and its purpose. I suggest that if the Lord so directs you, look up the original decree of your city at its inception. Find any poem or proclamation that has had major significance for the city. Also look up the meaning of the city's name and facts about its origin. You will probably recognize that the exact strongholds your city is fighting today are linked directly to these early decrees, poems and proclamations.

Mobile recently celebrated its 300th birthday. Dr. and Mrs. George Hall attend our church and they brought to my attention an old decree that had been written about the city. It was a negative and foreboding declaration that was more of a curse than a blessing. These prayer warriors began meeting to pray that our mayor would give us permission to write a new decree. I appealed to Mayor Dow for a new decree to be written and the old one to be revoked before the birthday festivities began.

Mayor Dow gave our intercessors permission and commissioned them to write it. The result is shown at the right:

When the mayor unveiled a new statue during the celebration of Mobile's 300th birthday, he read this new decree over our city. He also sealed it with the city seal and later read it on television and proclaimed it boldly. Today this decree hangs in the mayor's office, the Chamber of Commerce and the State Docks overlooking Mobile Bay.

Stewardship/Financial Decrees

You can write a stewardship/financial decree as King Artaxerxes did in Ezra 7. Here is another pagan king fulfilling God's Word by allowing Ezra the priest and a group of Jews to return to Jerusalem and begin rebuilding the Temple. Remember, we have a dual role—both kingly and priestly. In this story, a king and a priest worked together to fulfill God's will: The king wrote a stewardship/financial decree to build the house of God and the priest led the building effort.

It is in our kingly role that we are stewards of our finances. We are stewards of our work, our investments, our spending habits and our giving to the Lord. May I be honest with you? I have known many people who grew

Proclamation

WHEREAS, through the gateway of Mobile Bay, the technology designed by our sons and daughters is carried on the trade winds to the nations; our ship channel is forever crowded with vessels steaming toward our docks, dispersing their cargo – only to refill their massive hulls once again in this city that is the window to the world; and

WHEREAS, our great oaks and pines that stand tall and look skyward are only surpassed in their reach for the stars by our yearning and thriving workforce, prepared to climb to new heights in a new century of progress; and

WHEREAS, our rolling hills and valleys are never silent of the sound of hammer and nail as our craftsmen build dwellings for the teeming masses of adventurers who have come to find their fame and fortune in this city by the bay; and

WHEREAS, Mobile – three hundred years old – was once a sleepy city by the bay; now this city of destiny and port of entrance to the world is a competitor in the global marketplaces; and

WHEREAS, Mobile is a city unwilling to settle for the good when the best can be achieved – striving for the best in unity and equality in our citizenry, education, business and commerce, science and technology and in the protection of our natural resources; and

WHEREAS, a port city of refuge, Mobile is the birthplace of heroes and nurturer of legacies; her young and old shall fulfill their destinies; her bay shall continually surround her with safety; all who enter her gates shall find rest, joy and strength.

Done this 4th day of July, 2002, in the City of Mobile, Alabama.

Michael C. Dow
MAYOR

extreme in their desire to prosper. It was sad to see how the accumulation of wealth became everything to them. In a godly life, our kingly role and our priestly role are balanced. Yet some forget about their priestly ministry to Christ and to others. Usually they say, "Just give me two years. I'll get my business off the ground, I'll be financially secure and then, man, look what I can do for the Kingdom." I have never seen this business plan work. Usually they become so consumed in their quest for money that they forget about their spiritual calling.

So why not experience long-term prosperity, favor and blessing in the financial arena by writing down a stewardship/financial decree that describes your commitment to both your kingly role in the business marketplace and your priestly role in the ministry to God, your family and the Body of believers?

You can read King Artaxerxes' decree in Ezra 7:13–21. Here are the elements of his stewardship/financial decree:

First and foremost decree that your business and family finances will fully comply with the teaching of God's Word (verses 13–14).

Next decree that you will be a good steward of your finances: "You are to carry the silver and gold" (verse 15).

Decree that God will give your hands power to gain wealth: ". . . all the silver and gold that you may find in all the province of Babylon" (verse 16).

Commit to transfer the firstfruits of your income into Kingdom causes: "The silver and gold . . . are to be freely offered for the house of their God in Jerusalem" (verse 16).

Decree that you will not be bound by spending over your budget: "Now therefore, be careful to buy with this money" (verse 17).

After your freewill, firstfruits offering has been given to the Lord, decree that He will give you wisdom in investing the remaining amount: "And whatever seems good to you and your brethren to do with the rest of the silver and the gold, do it according to the will of your God" (verse 18).

Decree that you will never hold anything back that belongs to the Lord: "Also the articles that are given to you for the service of the house of your God, deliver in full before the God of Jerusalem" (verse 19).

And finally, decree that all the needs of your finances will be met: "And whatever more may be needed" (verse 20).

Now, as a trusted and faithful steward of God's wealth, fulfilling your kingly and priestly roles, you can decree an overflow of wealth into your storehouse. Because of your decree, God trusts that it will be invested diligently into His Kingdom's work. King Artaxerxes decreed in verse 21 that all of the treasuries in the regions surrounding Jerusalem would be open to pour into the house of God anything that Ezra the priest needed.

Word Decrees

There are more than thirty thousand promises in the Bible. You might say that these promises are God's written decrees. To write a Word decree, simply write down what God's Word says about a matter that is of concern to you. If you are concerned about your children, write down God's decrees about your children's future. If you are concerned about your health, write down decrees related to divine healing and so on.

We see this principle at work in the book of Esther. We saw earlier that Haman was an Amalekite—a descendant of the nation that attacked Israel as she left Egypt. Joshua and the Israelite army fought with Amalek in Rephidim as Aaron and Hur held up the hands of Moses on a hill above the battlefield.

After God brought the victory to Israel He said to Moses, "Write this for a memorial in the book and recount it in the hearing of Joshua, that I will utterly blot out the remembrance of Amalek from under heaven" (Exodus 17:14).

God commanded Moses to write a decree stating that He would wipe out the memory of Amalek, and then told Moses to recount it. Do you think there is any connection between this decree that Israel would be delivered from the Amalekites, and Mordecai's confidence that deliverance and enlargement would come regardless of Haman or the Amalekites' threats? I believe so. Writing the Word and recounting it is God's prescription for breakthrough living.

The children of Israel were instructed to write God's decrees "on the doorposts of your house and on your gates" (Deuteronomy 6:9). Today, Orthodox Jews continue this practice with the *mezuzah*, a small tube that holds the handwritten words of Deuteronomy 6:4–9 and 11:13–21 and is nailed to the doorposts of their homes. The mezuzah is hung on an angle so that the power of the Word is always flowing out to the community from their homes. A true Orthodox Jew will touch the mezuzah as he walks in and out of his door and then kiss the fingers that touched it in honor of and respect for God's Word. They write the Word and place it in the mezuzah so that they can recount it more easily.

As long as I can remember my home has always had a mezuzah on the doorpost. It is a constant reminder to me that my family and I are committed to obey God's Word inside and outside of our home.

Moses commanded the children of Israel that when they crossed the Jordan after their departure from Egypt, they had some writing to do before they entered the Promised Land.

> "And it shall be, on the day when you cross over the Jordan to the land which the LORD your God is giving you, that you shall set up for yourselves large stones, and whitewash them with lime. You shall write on them all the words of this law, when you have crossed over, that you may enter the land which the LORD your God is giving you."
>
> Deuteronomy 27:2–3

Today in Israel the Orthodox Jews still understand the power of the pen and they follow God's prescription to write and recount His Word. One of the things that has kept the Jews together through two thousand years of dispersion has been their practice of writing and recounting God's Word.

Life Vision Decrees

Habakkuk 2:2 says, "Write the vision and make it plain on tablets, that he may run who reads it." If you don't write down the vision, how will you know if it is being fulfilled? Your vision is your life's purpose and calling. A written vision is like a compass to you. When you begin to veer the vision always brings you back on course.

Someone once asked Helen Keller what was worse than being born blind. Her answer? "Having sight with no vision."

Jackie Patillo is the head of the gospel music department for Integrity Music and is a member of our church. Jackie and I grew up together in the same church in the San Francisco Bay area. Today she is a single mom and deals with all of the "stuff" of life single parents contend with. But Jackie has never veered from her life's vision. Early in her walk with Christ she, like Esther, wrote down a decree for her future. Jackie put her "vision decree" in the front of her Bible and she reads it every so often to make sure she is still on course.

Habakkuk says that if the vision is plain, then the one who reads it can run. A written life's vision decree will keep you in the race!

These ten decrees serve as examples to you. There are many more decrees you can write: building your spiritual house decrees (1 Chronicles 28:19; Ezra 5:13); restoration decrees to bring back things lost or stolen (Ezra 6:1–5); decrees for worship leaders (2 Chronicles 35:4); holiness decrees (Exodus 39:30; Daniel 6:25–26); and repentance decrees (Jonah 3:7–10).

Remember the process God gives for writing decrees from Job 22:27–28. First pray and receive God's direction, and then write your decree. Also, because decrees are powerful, you should never write a decree for someone else's hurt: "Woe to those who decree unrighteous decrees, who write misfortune, which they have prescribed" (Isaiah 10:1).

Now it is your turn. Or as "Pharaoh" Yul Brynner said in the movie version of *The Ten Commandments*, "So let it be written, so let it be done!"

11

THE ESTHER DECREE

Though I have never played the lottery, the name of the game has always intrigued me. Who came up with the name *lottery* anyway? What does it mean? Webster's Dictionary defines a lottery this way: "A drawing of lots in which prizes are distributed to the winners among persons buying a chance. An event or affair whose outcome is or seems to be determined by chance." The word *lot* is defined as "an object used as a counter in determining a question by chance. The use of lots as a means of deciding something by chance."

In the ancient East the casting of lots was a common practice. Lots were small pieces of stone, broken pieces of pottery or strips of wood. Each lot had names or numbers written on it. There were different ways of determining how the lots would be cast or thrown. In some cases they were cast on the ground, much like rolling dice. In other cases they were drawn from a box or a bag, hence the phrase *drawing lots*, much like the game of bingo. Other times lots were cast into folds of a garment, like the robes worn in those days, and shuffled around until one fell out. Lots were used to settle disputes, determine one's future direction and make choices.

The Jews did not believe in gambling or divination but they used lots extensively to find God's will. In Joshua 14–18 we read that lots were used to divide the Promised Land among the tribes of Israel. In Acts 1:24–26 the disciples cast lots to determine who would take the place of Judas.

Now I know what you are thinking: *What does the lottery have to do with the decree of Esther?* Well, a lot. In fact, I believe that this little word *lot* is the most important word in the entire book of Esther. Miss its significance and you miss the whole enchilada.

The word *lot* comes from the Hebrew word *pur*. We have seen that when Haman sought to destroy every last one of the Jews in the kingdom of Ahasuerus, he cast lots. Esther 3:7 states:

> In the first month, which is the month of Nisan, in the twelfth year of King Ahasuerus, they cast Pur (that is, the lot), before Haman to determine the day and the month, until it fell on the twelfth month, which is the month of Adar.

By casting the lot Haman determined when the Jews would die and accordingly put the day of their destruction in a written decree. Facing their sentence "there was great mourning among the Jews, with fasting, weeping, and wailing; and many lay in sackcloth and ashes" (Esther 4:3).

Even more horribly, the date was set for eleven months in the future, meaning the Jews would have to endure the gathering storm of hatred against them.

Predetermined Fate

Now here is the good part. The casting of the lot in the Persian culture was much more than a dice game that helped in decision-making or settling disputes. Philosophically, Persia was fatalistic and lots were cast to determine the outcome of not only the events in the kingdom but also one's own future. The belief in a predetermined fate was at the core of the culture in which Esther lived.

Haman without doubt believed that by casting Pur the fate of the Jews was sealed and there would be no changing it. Indeed the book of Esther is about the clashing of two systems of belief: fatalism and faith. Webster's defines *fatalism* this way: "The acceptance of all things and events as inevitable; the doctrine that all events are subject to fate or inevitable predetermination."

Fatalism is the belief that the game of life is fixed. A fatalist is passive about her ability to change her destiny. The whole theme of this book, "You can change your future through prophetic proclamation," is anathema to a fatalist. A fatalist accepts life as it is dished out. When faced with trying circumstances the fatalist throws up her hands and says, "There is no use trying to solve my issues and problems. My fate has already been predetermined."

Fatalism drains a person's hope and shatters his motivation. Fatalism denies that God's sovereign workings joined with human responsibility can change the course of our future.

Have you ever struggled with fatalism? I admit it: I have. But then I read the book of Esther and now I recognize the ugly tentacles of fatalism for what they really are: subtle branches of a life philosophy that opposes the providence and sovereignty of a God who is able to change my circumstances.

In direct contrast to fatalism, the doctrines of providence and sovereignty teach that a loving God holds my future in His hand and intervenes to help me in times of need.

When difficulties arise have you ever said the words "Well, that's just my lot in life"? Though you may be unaware, you have just proclaimed the mantra of the hardcore fatalist. However the lot has fallen in your lap is what your predetermined outcome will be. In other words, your future is set in stone, the mold has been cast, the die has been thrown, your bed has been made and now you must sleep in it. You can never break out of this mold because—"it's your lot in life." So says the fatalist.

Fatalism promotes a tragic vision of life. On the other hand, faith in the providence of a loving God frees us to, by faith, fulfill the destiny to which we are called. Through God's providence, I know I have authentic freedom by submitting my life to the guidance of the Holy Spirit.

The difference between fatalism and faith was made real to me as I walked the streets of Calcutta, India, on a Sunday morning a few years ago. Because of the many fatalistic religions in India that teach the acceptance of poverty, sickness and disease as one's lot in life, there are literally millions of people living on the streets under cardboard boxes or whatever they can find for shelter. They believe that if they submit to their lot and accept it as their fate, things will be much better in the next life after they are reincarnated.

Winding my way through this maze of affliction and suffering I found Mark Buntain Memorial Church where I was to preach. I was immediately captivated by the power of the cross of Jesus to transform a fatalist. By the cross, we know a God who reverses the curse and turns the tables. Here before me were thousands of beautiful Indian people worshiping their Savior and Deliverer. Many came from living on the streets I had just traveled. Many had received physical healing and were now employed and self-supporting.

Fatalism has crept into some Christian circles as well. There is a teaching that says, "Because the elect believers were chosen before the foundation of the world, there is no use sharing our faith with unbelievers. The elect have already been predetermined to be saved and will come to Christ whether we share with them or not." A fatalistic teaching indeed. The error of this teaching is that it undermines the responsibility of every believer to fulfill the Great Commission.

The Turning Point

Though it is not mentioned in the text, Haman probably went to his pagan temple and asked the priests or diviners to cast the lots for him. It is interesting that they cast these lots for Haman in the first month of the year, Nisan. Their fatalistic religion taught that the gods gathered in the new year to determine everyone's fate for that year. The date for the Jews' destruction fell on Adar 13, which on our calendar is March 13. For Haman this was an excellent day to kill the Jews because the Persians believed that the number 13 was a sign of misfortune or death.

It is also interesting that the day Haman cast lots and wrote a decree for the Jews' destruction, Nisan 13, was the day before the Passover (see Exodus 12:6). The Jews were not given over to the Persian cultural belief of fatalism. I believe that the remembrance of Passover just a day after their destruction was decreed gave them hope to say, "If God delivered us in the Passover from Pharaoh and the angel of death, then He can deliver us from Haman, too!"

Have you allowed the seeds of Haman's fatalism to be sown in your thinking? Have you come to the belief that your fate is sealed? Think again. No one knows his or her future. There is no set lot in life. A lucky draw or a favorable roll of the dice or the first lot to fall from the folds of a garment does not seal your fate.

Your future is in God's hands. Proverbs 16:33 says, "The lot is cast into the lap, but its every decision is from the LORD." Your fate has not been predetermined, you see. God can change your lot and turn the tables in your favor. Some challenging issues may be cast into your lap but the Lord determines the outcome.

Mordecai expressed his rejection of fatalism and his acceptance and faith in a sovereign God who held Israel's future in His hand. In Esther 4:14 he said, "Who knows whether you have come to the kingdom for such a time as this?" Found within this question are two more key words of the book of Esther: *Who knows?* By the casting of his fatalistic lots to predetermine Israel's demise, Haman said, "I know: Your future has been sealed." But Mordecai said, "No one knows: Our future is in God's hands."

Talk about poetic justice! By decree the Jews were given the right to defend themselves and they overpowered their enemies on the day of their planned annihilation, Adar 13.

> Now in the twelfth month, that is, the month of Adar, on the thirteenth day, the time came for the king's command and his decree to be executed. On the day that the enemies of the Jews had hoped to overpower them, the opposite occurred, in that the Jews themselves overpowered those who hated them. The Jews gathered together in their cities throughout all the provinces of King Ahasuerus to lay hands on those who sought their harm. And no one could withstand them, because fear of them fell upon all people. And all the officials of the provinces, the satraps, the governors, and all those doing the king's work, helped the Jews, because the fear of Mordecai fell upon them.
>
> Esther 9:1–3

Tables turned! Sentence reversed! Lots changed! All proving the error of fatalism and the security of trusting in a sovereign God. A verse that comes to mind is 2 Corinthians 5:17: "Therefore, if anyone is in Christ, he is a new creation; old things have passed away; behold, all things have become new."

The Judeo/Christian belief is anything but fatalistic. We believe in a God who is able to turn our mourning into dancing. We trust in a Savior who is willing not only to forgive but also to change our circumstances.

Fatalism, on the other hand, traces your woes and problems back to one event that turned all of your positives into negatives, mornings into evenings and springs into winters.

Fatalism says, "If my parents had been different; if my education had been better; if I had not committed that sin; or had the accident; or been abused; or gone through with the abortion; or made that miscalculation in my business; or left my spouse . . . then things would have turned out differently for me."

Fatalists look back into their pasts, find one event that started the downward spiral and conclude, "The lot has been cast, the die is set and now I'm stuck in a mold. I'll never change." Fatalists believe that because of a painful past event they have been sent to a Siberian labor camp and sentenced to twenty years of hard labor with no parole. They trudge hopelessly through life believing they are heading down a dead-end street with no way to change direction.

Everyone can look back on past life experiences and dredge up a negative. The difference is how we view the event. Fatalists see the event as the creator of a rut they cannot get out of. The person of faith looks back at the divorce, the accident, the rejection, the pain, the grief of sin and sees it as a turning point. The person of faith believes that there is no set lot in life. He believes that life may cast the lot into his lap but that God has the final word.

I have the privilege of pastoring an awesome church that is moving in new realms of worship, discipleship, evangelism and racial reconciliation. Darrell Williams is one of the incredible men of God in our church. In the 1988–89 school year, Darrell was the number-one-rated high school football player in the Southeastern United States. That year as a running back he set the Alabama state high school record with 5,559 yards and 54 touchdowns. His school that year, Viger High, was voted by ESPN as having the number-one high school football team in America.

As a college freshman, Darrell surpassed the senior players and led Auburn University in rushing and touchdowns and gained a spot on the Southeast Conference all-freshman team. Darrell was destined for a football career in the NFL, when a knee injury in his junior year ended his dream.

Instead of looking at this event through the eyes of a fatalist, Darrell saw it as God leading him sovereignly into a new life direction. He got his degree in criminal justice and worked six years as a juvenile parole officer and is now fulfilling his passion as a personal fitness trainer. The injury was to him a steppingstone into a new life purpose and calling rather than a fatalistic event that ruined his destiny.

The Amalek Lesson

Esther and the Jews also saw a chance to carve out a new destiny for themselves when it seemed that all was lost. We looked earlier at the fact that the Jews could trace their present suffering back to one defining moment in their nation's past. Had it not happened there would have been no gallows and no written decree against them.

Do you recall the event? It was when Israel came up out of Egypt and Amalek, a forefather of Haman, came to fight against them. Amalek attacked the weakest part of the sojourners, falling upon the women, children and old folks at the back of the line. After Joshua defeated Amalek and his hordes, God said to Moses, "Write this for a memorial in the book and recount it in the hearing of Joshua, that I will utterly blot out the remembrance of Amalek from under heaven" (Exodus 17:14).

Many years later when Saul was anointed to be king over Israel, the prophet Samuel gave him this command from the Lord:

"Thus says the LORD of hosts: 'I will punish what Amalek did to Israel, how he laid wait for him on the way when he came up from Egypt. Now go and attack Amalek, and utterly destroy all that they have, and do not spare them.'"

1 Samuel 15:2–3

But Saul and the people of Israel spared Agag, the king of the Amalekites, and took the best of the plunder, including the livestock. They probably figured, What could be wrong with the sheep and oxen? But God had commanded them to destroy everything.

Samuel inquired of Saul, "Why . . . did you not obey the voice of the LORD? Why did you swoop down on the spoil, and do evil in the sight of the LORD?" (1 Samuel 15:19). Then came Samuel's famous words to King Saul:

> "Behold, to obey is better than sacrifice, and to heed than the fat of rams. For rebellion is as the sin of witchcraft, and stubbornness is as iniquity and idolatry. Because you have rejected the word of the LORD, He also has rejected you from being king."

1 Samuel 15:22–23

In Esther's day the Amalekites were still alive and well because of Saul's disobedience. If Saul had obeyed God there would not have been a Haman, a noose or a decree of destruction. If Mordecai and Esther were fatalists they would have believed that their lot was already cast and their fate was sealed and that they could do nothing to reverse the curse of Haman.

Instead they believed that deliverance and enlargement were on the way. A person of faith always believes, "This could be the day when my deliverance comes." Faith teaches us that it is only a matter of time before the tables will be turned on our behalf. A person who has overcome a fatalistic mindset refuses to conclude that a past mistake can halt his future progress.

What happened on Adar 13 and 14 was really incredible. Not only did the Jews defeat their attackers but they broke free from the chains of their past. This time when they fought the Amalekites they refused to touch the spoils of battle as Saul and their fathers had done. Three times it is mentioned in the ninth chapter of Esther that "they did not lay a hand on the plunder" (verses 10, 15–16), thus freeing themselves from the bondage of a past sin.

Breaking the Curse

Something else happened that day that shows the hand of God moving behind the scenes to free us from past mistakes. There is a verse in the book of Esther that I missed even after reading it several times. Here is Esther 2:5: "In Shushan the citadel there was a certain Jew whose name was Mordecai the son of Jair, the son of Shimei, the son of Kish, a Benjamite."

Did you catch it? Mordecai and his uncle's daughter, Esther, were both Benjamites from the house and lineage of King Saul. God had orchestrated the events of history so that two people from Saul's very household would lead the charge in breaking the generational curse of Saul's rebellion and sin.

Furthermore, this man Shimei, mentioned in Mordecai's genealogy, was the same man from the family of the house of Saul who cursed King David when his son Absalom tried to take over his kingdom. In his cursing Shimei proclaimed that the Lord had delivered the throne of David into the hand of another. This curse flew smack in the face of the Messianic promise that the throne of David would be established forever. Thus, not only did Mordecai and Esther—two Benjamites—break the generational curse of Saul's rebellion, they also by their written decree prevented a massacre that would have destroyed the Messianic seed. They broke the generational curse of their forefather Shimei.

At the end of the day on Adar 13 there was one order of business left undone. Esther appealed to the king one more time, this time for the bodies of the ten sons of Haman, who had been killed in the slaughter, to be displayed on the same gallows where their father was hanged. You can read their names in Esther 9:7–9.

Some say that Esther was cold and calculating because she asked the king for the public display of the bodies of Haman's sons. On the contrary, wise Esther knew that you could never appease the adversary of your soul. She was committed to remove any last vestige of the spirit of Haman from the threat of her people.

The ten sons had some interesting Persian names. Their English translations are telling. *Parshandatha* means "meddler" or "busybody"; *Dalphon* means "self-pity"; *Aspatha* means "self-sufficient"; *Poratha* means "self-indulgent"; *Adalia* means "inferiority" or "self-conscious"; *Aridatha* means "strong self-will"; *Parmashta* means "preeminent self" or "competitive"; *Arisai* means "imprudent self"; *Aridai* means "proud," "haughty," "superior"; and *Vajezatha* means "self-righteous."

On Adar 13 and 14, Esther not only broke away from her generational curses but she also dealt ruthlessly with the nagging issues in her present. She held firmly to the faith conviction that no past mistake or present bondage is outside a sovereign God's ability to turn around.

Having gathered together on Adar 13 and 14 to defend themselves against those still bent on their destruction, the Jews killed 75,000 of their attackers. The Jews did not suffer one casualty. To commemorate their victory Mordecai wrote letters to all the Jews in the 127 provinces of Persia that they should

> celebrate yearly the fourteenth and fifteenth days of the month of Adar, as the days on which the Jews had rest from their enemies, as the month which was turned from sorrow to joy for them, and from mourning to a holiday; that they should make them days of feasting and joy, of sending presents to one another and gifts to the poor.
>
> Esther 9:21–22

Reversal of Misfortune

Because Haman had fatalistically cast Pur to determine the day of their destruction, what do you suppose the Jews called these two days of celebration? Purim: the lot! It would be the same as if you took one of the worst things that ever happened to you and made it the title of an annual day of celebration. Only people who trust in a sovereign God have this ability. Romans 8:28 comes to mind: "And we know that all things work together for good to those who love God, to those who are the called according to His purpose."

When God turns the tables on the adversary on your behalf and you experience deliverance and enlargement, you could call your special day "cancer" or "depression" or "worry." How about "pain" or "rejection" or "divorce proceedings," even "job termination." It is a bold move, I know, but it is a description of the painful lot that was cast into your lap and a remembrance of its reversal, your subsequent healing, deliverance and promotion.

But why not just celebrate the holiday of Purim with the Jews? Esther was so committed to the holiday that she wrote a second letter with Mordecai to confirm the Purim celebration and to decree its continuation for coming generations:

> That these days should be remembered and kept throughout every generation, every family, every province, and every city, that these days of Purim should not fail to be observed among the Jews, and that the memory of them should not perish among their descendants. . . . So the decree of Esther confirmed these matters of Purim, and it was written in the book.
>
> Esther 9:28, 32

Notice the words of verse 32: "The decree of Esther confirmed these matters of Purim." There are several decrees in the book of Esther, but only one is called "the decree of Esther," and it was written to establish the Feast of Purim. Based on her written decree, Purim has been observed ever since. Many Bible scholars believe Purim was the feast that Jesus attended in John 5:1. Today Jews all around the world celebrate the Purim holiday in late February or early March.

Remember, *purim* is the Hebrew word for *lots* in commemoration of the Pur cast by Haman. *Purim* is also known as the "Feast of Esther." During the celebration on Adar 14 and 15, a handwritten *Megillah* or "scroll" of the book of Esther is read in every Jewish home observing the feast. Through the reading, each listener hears once again the awesome story of God's faithfulness.

I am of Jewish descent. Recently my wife, Sharon, and I were visiting my cousins in Israel and stepped into a silver shop in Jerusalem to browse for gifts. On one wall were shelves filled with a number of tubes of different heights, anywhere from 12 to 24 inches. Most were quite ornamental in design. I asked the shop owner what these containers were and she looked at me with a startled gaze as if to say, "You don't know?" She took one off the shelf and pointed out the writing in Hebrew that graced the container's side. The words read, "The Scroll of Esther." Go into any observant Jewish home today anywhere in the world and you will find such a thing. Needless to say one graces my desk today.

My Israeli family is having a rabbinical scribe write the scroll of Esther by hand for me. They tell me a copy is not kosher. Go figure!

As the scroll is being read on the night of Purim in the synagogue and in the homes, whenever the name Haman is mentioned the celebrants make noises, stomp their feet, and clang pots and pans together. Others use hand-held noisemakers called groggers to drown out Haman's name when it is read. Some even write the name of Haman on the soles of their shoes and stomp their feet in order to blot out his name, because God desired to erase or blot out the memory of Amalek. Others write Haman's name in wax and melt it. The Feast of Purim is also filled with special food, the most popular being the Hamantashen pastries.

Oftentimes the story of Esther is acted out in skits. Again, when Haman's name is mentioned those watching the play will shout *venahafoch hu,* which means "the opposite happened." The Feast of Purim is the most joyous of all Jewish holidays. It is a celebration of the reversal of misfortune into blessing.

THE DECREE OF ESTHER

In 1941 Adolf Hitler banned Jews in Poland from reading the scroll of Esther during the Purim holiday and closed the synagogues to make sure. He blamed all the problems in Germany on "international Jewry" and stated, "If we don't successfully annihilate the Jews, they will be able to celebrate another Purim." As we know, Hitler committed suicide and his ten henchmen (any link to Haman's ten sons?) were found guilty in the Nuremberg trials in 1946, during the Purim holiday. As the ten Nazis were hanged on the gallows, one of them, Julius Streicher, shouted, "Purimfest!" Perhaps he realized the significance of the reversal of Hitler's proclamation to end the feast of Purim and that he was getting his just reward.

It's Our Time

The book of Esther beautifully blends together God's sovereignty and man's responsibility. God in His sovereignty orchestrated Esther's rise from obscurity and brought her to the kingdom at the exact moment in time that her influence would be needed.

Esther, for her part, showed responsibility. She submitted to the beauty process and the myrrh anointing, walked in two-dimensional obedience and favor, approached the king with a godly appeal and then wrote a new decree that protected and saved the Jews.

I have said throughout this book that Esther is a prophetic book for a prophetic time. It is a blueprint for what God is accomplishing in our generation. The Jewish book the *Medrash* declares that the Feast of Purim will be the highest and most practiced holiday in the time of the Messiah. There is also a belief in Judaism that the book of Esther will be the only book read during Messiah's reign.

Speaking of the Messiah, there is an interesting chorus sung in the synagogue during the Feast of Purim and here are its words: *Utzu etzah, vetufar; dabru davar, velo yakum; ki Immanuel.* These words are from Isaiah 8:10 and prophetically speak about the rise of the antichrist spirit against God's children in the last days. The translation is, "Take counsel together, but it will come to nothing; speak the word, but it will not stand, for God is with us." Wonderfully, the Hebrew word for God here in Isaiah 8:10 is *Immanuel*—the one prophesied to be born of a virgin in Isaiah 7:14—our Messiah Jesus, Immanuel, God with us!

At Jesus' cross His Father reversed the curse and turned an instrument of death into an instrument of life on our behalf. When I truly encounter the power of His cross my life is forever changed. Now, every time we receive the cup and the bread, we do it in remembrance of His sacrifice.

Esther wrote a decree commanding that we remember the reversing of the lots. Jesus commanded us to remember that on the cross He reversed the lots cast into our laps. In Esther, the memory of Haman was forever blotted out. In Jesus the memory of our sin is forever blotted out.

Yes, the lottery does have a lot to do with the book of Esther. When the lots were cast against Esther she spent three days in fasting and emerged to stand in her royal robe under the scepter of favor held in the king's right hand. He offered her up to half his kingdom. After the lots were cast against Jesus by the Roman soldiers who gambled for His robe, He spent three days in the tomb and emerged victorious. He is now seated in a robe of righteousness at the Father's right hand of favor, forever ready to give to you the keys of His Kingdom. And with those keys, you can bind or loose any lot cast against you.

Many believe that the three days Esther spent in fasting and the three days Jesus spent in the tomb are the same days in the Jewish calendar. That would not surprise me at all.

Dear one, we are entering into days such as the world has never seen before. We know from Scripture that the future will be filled with perplexity. An antichrist-like Haman spirit is rising against God's people the world over. It would be easy to become fatalistic as we face the prospects of our Haman and bow to him at the gate.

The antichrist spirit of Amalek is on the rise against the people of God, but the promise of God to Moses in Exodus 17:14 still stands secure: "I will utterly blot out the remembrance of Amalek from under heaven." This murderous spirit continues to raise its ugly head toward God's Kingdom purpose and His Kingdom people. Young Esther interceded before the king, and not only did Haman the Amalekite fall, but his ten sons as well.

I said earlier that the title given the king of Persia was *Ahasuerus*, which means "father." The king had another title as well: *Xerxes*. Want to know what it means? "Lion, king of heroes, king of kings"! Ahasuerus serves, then, as a double type of God the Father and His Son, Jesus Christ. Interestingly Isaiah prophesies that the Messiah Himself will be an "Everlasting Father" (Isaiah 9:6).

Beloved, it is time for the Esther intercessors to rise up in this generation and stand in unity before the King. As we do, the Lion of the tribe of Judah will blot out every last vestige of the antichrist spirit and destroy the foundations of his ten kingdoms the Bible says will rise in the last days. You can be sure that one day soon the loud angelic announcement will declare, "The kingdoms of this world have become the kingdoms of our Lord and of His Christ"

(Revelation 11:15). The scepter of King Jesus—the Lion, the King of heroes, the King of kings—is being raised in power toward every heroic Esther who will dare to be anointed with myrrh and stand up prayerfully against the Haman-like spirit in our generation, believing that "the destruction decreed shall overflow with righteousness" (Isaiah 10:22).

This is your moment to shine. Wherever you are in the beauty process—in the bitter myrrh or in the sweet-smelling perfumes—please know that Christ's ultimate desire is to make you a glorious Bride like Esther whom He displays to the world in this generation. He is not returning for a downtrodden, fatalistic Church but for a "glorious church, not having spot or wrinkle or any such thing" (Ephesians 5:27).

Who knows whether you have come to the Kingdom for such a time as this?

Aaron Früh was born and raised in the San Francisco Bay area. His father was killed by a drunk driver when he was three years old. He and his sister, Kathy, were reared by a very brave single mother named Nora.

Aaron earned an M.A. in educational ministries from Wheaton College. He is the senior pastor of Knollwood Church in Mobile, Alabama. He and his wife, Dr. Sharon Früh, have four children: Rachel, Elizabeth, Hannah and Nathan.

Aaron has traveled extensively in overseas missions and is currently involved in medical humanitarian projects in Israel. He has been a regular host on the regional TBN affiliate. His favorite pastime is having a good cup of morning coffee with Sharon on their back patio.

If you would like to be in touch with Aaron, you can contact him through

Knollwood Church
1501 Knollwood Dr.
Mobile, AL 36609
(251) 661-8383
afruh@bellsouth.net